What the experts are saying about *KidShape Café*...

"I highly recommend this unique recipe book with quick, easily prepared, healthy recipes to parents, children, pediatricians, nutritionists, family physicians, teachers, and exercise therapists. It contains all they need to know about shopping and preparing healthy meals and snacks that kids enjoy eating. These recipes are so easy that children and teens will have fun making their own meals and snacks.

> —**Juanita A. Archer**, MS, MD
> Emeritus Associate Professor of Endocrinology, College of Medicine,
> Howard University

"Often I feel like I am trying desperately to save a child from drowning in an ocean of foods wrapped in plastic wrappers. Finally I have been thrown a life raft. What a delight! Delicious foods, freshly prepared! Thank you, Dr. Neufeld."

> —**Chris Landon** MD, FAAP, FCCP, CMD
> Executive Director, Landon Pediatric Foundation; Director of Pediatrics,
> Ventura County Medical Center, Ventura, California

"*KidShape Café* is an informative, useful guide for families who want to have their children eat healthy. The guides in this book for how to serve and eat healthy portions are easy to use, and the recipes are kid-pleasing and terrific!"

> —**Debra Counts**, MD
> Pediatric Endocrinologist and Associate Professor of Pediatrics

"I would recommend this book to any family looking for ways to help the overweight and obese children they love."

> —**David Heber**, MD, PhD
> Professor of Medicine and Director, UCLA Center for Human Nutrition;
> author of *The L.A. Shape Diet*

"This book gives tips on portion sizes and contains excellent recipes that will appeal to children as well as the adults in the family. The advice provides an achievable commonsense approach to healthier eating and is an excellent addition to the cookbook collection of all parents who wish to implement healthy eating in their households.

—Janet Silverstein, MD
Professor and Chief, Pediatric Endocrinology, University of Florida

"*KidShape Café* is much more than an outstanding collection of easy, healthy, kid-tested recipes—it's a complete guide to healthy living for kids and the grownups who love them."

—Rose Schneier, MD, FAAP, FACE
Director, Division of Endocrinology and Diabetes,
Children's Hospital of Austin

"The most important gift that a parent can give to a child is the gift of a long, healthy life. In this marvelous book Dr. Neufeld provides good advice and tasty menus, giving parents and their children the recipe for healthy living."

—Donald Bergman, MD
President-Elect, American College of Endocrinology; Past President,
American Association of Clinical Endocrinologists; Clinical Professor of
Medicine, Mount Sinai School of Medicine, New York, New York

"*KidShape Café* is a terrific book, providing practical tips and appealing kid-tested recipes for the entire family. Highly recommended to everyone wanting to adopt healthier eating habits for life."

—John Foreyt, PhD
Director, Behavioral Medicine Research Center, Baylor College of Medicine

NAOMI NEUFELD, MD, FACE

WITH SARA J. HENRY

RECIPES BY DAVID LAWRENCE

RUTLEDGE HILL PRESS
Nashville, Tennessee
A Division of Thomas Nelson Publishers
Since 1798

www.thomasnelson.com

Published by Rutledge Hill Press, a Division of Thomas Nelson, Inc., P.O. Box 141000, Nashville, Tennessee 37214.

Rutledge Hill Press books may be purchased in bulk for educational, business, fundraising, or sales promotional use. For information, please e-mail SpecialMarkets@ThomasNelson.com.

KidShape® Registered U.S. Patent and Trademark Office.

Some of the material in this book has been adapted from *The KidShape Student Workbook, The KidShape Parent Workbook,* and the *KidShape Program Manual,* copyright © 2003, 2002, 2001, 1999, 1998, 1997 by the KidShape Foundation. This material has been adapted with the permission of the KidShape Foundation.

The information in this book is for general knowledge only. Before beginning any diet or exercise program, consult with your child's health care provider, as well as your own health care provider. Seek prompt medical care for any specific medical problem or concern.

Library of Congress Cataloging-in-Publication Data

Neufield, Naomi, 1947–
    Kidshape cafe / Naomi Neufield, with Sara J. Henry ; recipes by David Lawrence.
        p. cm.
    Includes index.
   ISBN 1-4016-0187-1 (trade paper)
   1. Obesity in children—Prevention. 2. Reducing diets—Recipes. 3. Cookery. I. Henry, Sara J. II. Lawrence, David, 1972– III. Title.
RJ399.C6N485 2005
641.5'63'083—dc22   2005019675

Printed in the United States of America
05 06 07 08 09 — 5 4 3 2 1

With love as always to Tim, whose faith in me allowed me to go beyond what I thought was possible and to achieve the dreams only he knew were there.

To my daughters, Pamela and Katherine, who have always been my best supporters as well as my best critics, and who have grown up to be role models for me.

To my parents, Maya and Dilip Das, for their love and support and for encouraging me to do my best.

Contents

Acknowledgments

Arriving at this point in the writing of a book like this, which requires so much effort from so many, can be both gratifying and intimidating because of the possibility of forgetting to thank someone for a valuable contribution.

My greatest thanks are to Christiane Wert Rivard, MPH, RD, program director of KidShape for more than 10 years, for her tireless effort and dedication to KidShape, as well as her unstinting and unselfish contributions to this book. Without her efforts and hard work this project would not have been possible.

This book also would not have been possible without David Lawrence and his creative energy and skill in making healthy foods appealing to children.

Another thank you goes to Heather Horowitz, RD, for her exhaustive efforts in completing the nutritional analyses, and for designing the appealing daily meal plans for families.

I am grateful to the KidShape students, past and present, and their families for sharing their insights and their recipes during our classes. They helped establish the need for the recipes and advice on healthy eating contained in this book.

Additionally, thanks to the people who gave me critical input vital to this book. Cheryl Forberg, RD, provided unselfish advice and suggestions at the start of this project. David Heber, MD, PhD, medical director of the UCLA Center for Human Nutrition, offered medical advice and his boundless energy, and was a great role model. My daughter Pam Neufeld, a talented writer, helped me in the development of this book.

I am especially grateful to the KidShape Foundation for the use of materials from the current and past workbooks, as well as to Gordon Stone and Jackie Morey for savvy advice.

Thank you to the wonderful people at Rutledge Hill Press for making this dream a reality. I am grateful to Sara Henry for her methodical and critical analysis while organizing this book, as well as to Jennifer Greenstein for her sharp eye and skillful prodding in editing the book. I am especially grateful to Larry Stone for everything that he has done for both this book and for KidShape.

Finally, I wish to offer a special thank you to Sandra Shagat of Zachary Shuster Harmsworth Literary Agency for her sage advice and encouragement in all aspects of this project.

PREFACE

I know how you feel about your children's health—because besides being a pediatric endocrinologist (and one of the first research physicians to identify the increase in type 2 diabetes among overweight children), I've raised two daughters. I also helped found KidShape, which is one of the most effective treatment programs for childhood obesity in the country and has helped more than 10,000 children and their families. KidShape is not a diet, but a healthy lifestyle that includes eating nutritious foods in moderation, exercising regularly, and developing a positive body image.

You hold in your hand *KidShape Café,* a cookbook with more than 150 kid-tested recipes that will help your entire family lose weight, stay healthy, and enjoy eating food that is as nutritious as it is tasty. *KidShape Café* is the answer you've been looking for. It also contains the six keys to healthy eating that we teach at KidShape and suggestions to help you incorporate them into your family. Putting these keys into practice will change your family's life and health. They will help you be an inspiration, an example, and a motivator for your children.

As medical director of KidShape, my passion is your child's good health. Chef David Lawrence and I have included as many great recipes and as much good advice as we can fit in this book. But if you have a question about something we don't cover, write me at ndneufeld@kidshape.com.

Chapter 1

What's a Parent to Do?

You love your children. You want what's best for them. You know they need to form good habits of eating and exercise that will give them a lifetime of good health. But it's not easy.

Every step of the way, you're battling not only long-standing habits but also a barrage of powerful outside influences. Budget cuts in schools have reduced the amount of physical education your child receives. Television ads tout candy, sugar-coated cereal, and high-fat microwave meals. Fast-food restaurants entice your kids with toys, play rooms, and fattening and appealing meals. Between TV, video games, and school activities, your child gets little exercise. Your own schedule is rushed, and when dinnertime comes around it's difficult enough to get food on the table without trying to plan a healthy menu your kids will eat.

Other families are facing the same pressures. More kids than ever before are overweight—and children who are overweight are more likely to face serious health problems such as asthma, type 2 diabetes, and a host of other medical problems. Every day in my medical practice I see children *as young as three years old* who are extremely ill from obesity. I notice a number of common factors among these

KIDSHAPE: HOW IT ALL STARTED

More than 20 years ago I began to see an increasing number of overweight children in my pediatric endocrinology practice. These children were referred to me because they had abnormal weight gain, early puberty, or acanthosis nigricans, a skin condition often associated with type 2 diabetes. I was one of the first doctors to realize that these children did not just have a glandular imbalance—their obesity was a contributing cause of their medical problems.

In 1986 my colleagues at Cedars Sinai Medical Center and I set up a family-based weight management program. It was the first such program to use the power of the entire family—centered around the family table—to bring about permanent change. Principles of family therapy had been applied to other behavioral problems, but no one had tried it with diet. And it worked! With the encouraging support of the family, even a seriously overweight child can adopt a healthy lifestyle and attain a healthy weight.

KidShape is a nine-week program for overweight children and their families. KidShape classes are taught by registered dietitians, who explain nutrition and healthy eating; by physical activity instructors, who exercise with the children and their parents; and by mental health professionals, who discuss the emotional aspects of overeating and the value of positive self-esteem. Of nearly 5,000 participants in KidShape programs, 87% of the children lost weight, and 80% of those children kept the weight off for at least two years.

KidShape opened with one site in Los Angeles County and later another site in Ventura County, just north of Los Angeles. Today the program is offered through more than 20 sites in southern California, and additional sites are licensed in western Pennsylvania, Philadelphia, northern California, New Mexico, and Texas.

The KidShape program was initially designed for children ages 6 to 14. In response to demand, we have developed KinderShape for younger children ages 3 to 5, and TeenShape for teens up to 19 years old. Because of the rich cultural diversity in the Los Angeles area, we have developed these programs in Spanish and Vietnamese as well as English. My 2004 book *KidShape* explains in detail how to implement the KidShape lessons at home. For more information, visit the KidShape Web site at www.kidshape.com.

children: most do not exercise, most rarely eat dinner with their families, and most eat far too much fast food, candy, and soft drinks.

What's a parent to do?

The KidShape Solution

It's important to realize that the obesity crisis didn't just happen. Our health-hostile world sabotages efforts to build a healthy lifestyle. Children become addicted to the sweet taste in sugar and high-fructose corn syrup and to the fats in fried food, and can struggle their entire lives to overcome that addiction and lose weight. It's not easy to instill in your children a love of nutritious food, the joy of a healthy lifestyle, and a passion for exercise, because our world is becoming increasingly health-hostile.

But you have the power to protect your children. You can help them develop the habit of movement and exercise. You can set a powerful example and help your children love healthy eating and develop a positive self-image. And you can teach them to make wise choices and give them healthy alternatives to the unhealthy foods that have become second nature. These are the principles of the KidShape program. KidShape is not a diet, but a lifestyle that focuses on healthy eating, exercise, and positive self-image.

Now more than ever, your children need your good advice and good example.

KidShape Café provides recipes, tips, and instructions that will help you prepare appealing and nutritious breakfasts, desserts, snacks, and dinners designed for all family members, whether overweight, underweight, or normal weight. It will help build a habit of healthy eating and start your children on a lifetime of good health. While it will take more planning to prepare these meals than stopping at a fast-food restaurant or tossing a pizza in the microwave, this is time invested in your children's health and their future.

And your kids are worth it.

Our Health-Hostile World

Face it! The environment surrounding your kids is relentless. Fast food seduces us with its easy availability and bargain prices. Restaurants ply us with portions much larger than we need. Junk food advertisements barrage us with images of tempting but unhealthy foods. Sugar in its many forms frequently constitutes the first or second ingredient in foods that are sometimes promoted as healthy.

I always take with a bit of skepticism reminiscences about "the good old days," but our past does look rosy when you compare it with the health-hostile world of the present. Today we have to work harder than ever before to keep our children healthy. Here are some reasons.

SCHOOLS ARE MORE HEALTH-HOSTILE. "Schools have become an unsafe nutrition environment," says Kelly Brownell, director of the Yale Center for Eating and Weight Disorders. High-sugar and high-calorie soda and junk food are more readily available in many schools than fruits and vegetables. Some schools serve franchised fast food in the cafeteria. Some schools have eliminated recess, and few states require regular physical education. In 1969 four of five kids played sports every day, while today only one in five does.

RESTAURANTS ARE MORE HEALTH-HOSTILE. Restaurants encourage us to eat more and the food they promote is less healthy. The U.S. Department of Health and Human Services reports that the increase in the average portion size is staggering compared to 20 years ago. Take a look at the calories in the average serving of these foods compared to 20 years ago:

	CALORIES THEN	CALORIES NOW
Bagel	140	350
Cheeseburger	333	590
Spaghetti	500	1,025
Soda	85	250
French fries	210	610
Turkey sandwich	320	820

INGREDIENTS IN FOODS ARE MORE HEALTH-HOSTILE. High-fructose corn syrup is probably the most common ingredient that makes us fat, and it shows up in places you would never expect. It's the number one ingredient in Hershey's Chocolate Syrup, but you'll also find it in ketchup, bottled iced tea, spaghetti sauce, and even bread and English muffins. High-fructose corn syrup is cheap, so manufacturers use a lot of it. Our consumption of high-fructose corn syrup climbed from zero in 1966 to one pound per year in 1972 to a whopping 62.6 pounds per person in 2001. Some researchers believe that (because of the way your body processes it) high-fructose corn syrup contributes to health problems such as obesity or even cancer.

COMMUNITY AND HOME ARE MORE HEALTH-HOSTILE. Twenty years ago Americans did 43% of their errands on foot; today we walk for only 25% of our errands. That's in part because we live in communities that encourage us to use the car rather than walk. Only 17% of children walk to school today, and by age 17 the average child has spent 38% more time in front of a television set than in school. And your metabolism is actually lower when sitting in front of a television set—resulting in fewer calories burned—than when sitting in the same chair reading a book. Another big factor in the rising epidemic of childhood obesity is the death of family mealtime. When a child eats alone, he or she is not likely to eat healthy food when processed, prepared foods (usually high in fat and low in fiber and important nutrients) are so easy to heat in the microwave.

What's a parent to do when faced with a health-hostile world?

It's up to you to protect your children. And *KidShape Café* contains the recipes, explanations, and tips you need to help you combat the health-hostile world and win.

Exercise—It's Not a Four-Letter Word

The word *exercise* may conjure up images of painfully jogging around the block or of being chosen last for teams, jeered at for being fat, and generally made miserable in physical education classes or recess.

You need to reinvent the word for you and your family—you need to make exercise fun. This can be as simple as playing a game of tag or badminton in the backyard, going sledding or roller-skating, or taking a short hike with a (healthy, of course) picnic at the end. Realize that if you or your child is overweight and hasn't done any exercise for a long time other than playing video games on the computer, you'll have to ease into this. It's crucial, especially at first, that sessions are short and your child doesn't get overtired or frustrated. Experiment to find activities that you can do together, as well as ones your child may want to pursue on his own.

Exercise is intrinsic to being healthy and maintaining a good body weight. Our bodies were made to move. Being active will give you more energy and improve your mood, and reduce stress as well. You won't immediately see the long-term benefits of exercise, but they're there: You're reducing the risks of diabetes, heart problems, and other diseases, and helping build strong bones and lungs.

Choose some physical activity options, and work them into your daily schedule—aim for a minimum of 20 minutes a day. Consider posting a chart on your refrigerator, where every family member enters daily activities. Eventually exercise will be so much a part of your daily life that you won't need to keep track, but for now, consider it an accomplishment that should be displayed.

Helping Your Child Feel Secure

A healthy body image and a healthy self-esteem are connected. If your child has a negative opinion about his or her body, it can have a negative impact on ego. Without body pride, people tend to make less of an effort to eat healthily and exercise.

If your child is overweight, he or she likely doesn't feel good about it. What can you do?

Something as simple as helping your child select flattering clothing, a new haircut, or a new pair of shoes can help. Praise your child for accomplishments and don't dwell on the negative.

Never let your child feel hungry and don't admonish your child about being overweight. Stress the value of good health and smart choices; serve healthy meals and keep nutritious snacks on hand.

The KidShape Keys to Healthy, Happy Eating

These six keys to healthy eating will help lead you and your children toward a lifetime of good health.

1. EAT REGULARLY. Many people actually lose weight by eating more often! When we're really hungry, we're more likely to overeat, and healthy snacks help keep blood sugar steady and avoid that "starving" feeling. This doesn't mean it is okay to graze all day: Keep a regular schedule of three meals and two healthy snacks daily. Don't let your children skip breakfast—it's your child's most important meal, and studies show that kids who skip breakfast are more likely to be overweight. Serve meals with lean protein that will help your children feel full longer and make them less likely to overeat. (You'll find many snack ideas in Chapter 5.)

2. CHOOSE HEALTHY DRINKS. Children fill up on empty calories in soda, fruit drinks, sports drinks, and even pure juice—all these are loaded with sugar, natural and added (some juice drinks are sweetened with high-fructose corn syrup). Decreasing high-sugar drinks and juice has been shown to help avoid childhood obesity. Skip all but pure juice, and limit that to four ounces per day. Water and low-fat or nonfat milk are much better choices. Children ages 2 to 8 should have two cups a day of milk or equivalent milk products to help build strong bones and teeth, and kids older than 9 should have three cups a day. (Note: Children under age 2 should have regular milk, never low-fat or nonfat.) Adults should remember that coffee and alcohol are diuretics, meaning that they take water out of your body. (See "Drink, Drink, Drink" on page 23.)

3. EAT YOUR FRUITS OR VEGETABLES. Fruits and vegetables are loaded with vitamins, fiber, and other nutrients, plus they're low in fat and calories, with no cholesterol. In short, fruits and vegetables have the good stuff we all need without any of the bad stuff we don't. Different colored fruits and vegetables are high in different vitamins and minerals, so choose fruits and vegetables in a variety of colors. Adults and children over age 2 should eat five to nine servings of fruits and vegetables every day. (Starchy vegetables such as potatoes count as grains or carbohydrates, not as vegetables.) For tips on getting your kids to eat more fruits and vegetables, see pages 155 and 166.

4. CHOOSE REASONABLE PORTION SIZES. Even if your children don't eat Hardee's Monster Thickburgers with their two-thirds of a pound of beef, four strips of bacon, and three slices of cheese—delivering 1,420 calories and 107 grams of fat—they most likely eat too much. One of the eye-opening exercises at KidShape is measuring food portions and learning that a serving size of whole-grain cereal is one cup instead of a full bowl and that a serving of peas is half a cup. (See "Determining Portion Sizes" on page 14.) If your kids are used to over-large portions, use smaller plates so family members won't feel deprived.

5. MAKE HEALTHY FOOD CHOICES. Empower your kids to help make healthier choices by learning to read food labels. We need to know what we are eating and you can find out by reading the label on the back of a jar or box—not the advertising promotion on the front! (See "Understanding Food Labels" on page 8.) Also pay attention to lists of ingredients on labels, and look for whole grains such as brown rice and

UNDERSTANDING FOOD LABELS

All manufacturers are required to list basic nutrition facts on a food label, and you can find valuable information here. And if your child is old enough to read, he or she can learn to read labels as well.

SERVING SIZE. Your favorite cereal may look as if it's low in calories, but take a close look at the serving size. A serving may be half a cup, and you may be regularly serving a cup or even more. (In fact, it's a good idea to carefully measure foods so you don't overserve.)

CALORIES FROM FAT. The closer this number is to the number of calories per serving, the fattier the food.

PERCENT DAILY VALUES. You can view these only as a rough guideline, because they are based on government recommendations for someone who eats 2,000 calories a day. Your children will likely be eating much less than this.

TOTAL FAT, SUGAR, PROTEIN. The label will also tell you the amounts (in grams) of fat, sugar, and protein. You'll know from your child's doctor or from the "Calorie Needs" chart on page 13 approximately how much fat, sugar, and protein your child should be eating daily.

DIETARY FIBER. Fiber is important for gastrointestinal health (and it helps your child feel full). To find the minimum recommended amount for your child, add five to his or her age: This means a six-year-old would need a minimum of 11 grams (6 plus 5) of dietary fiber daily. (Most children do not eat enough fiber.)

Also review the list of ingredients on the item's label, which are always listed in order. If high-fructose corn syrup is first on the list, the food you're considering has more corn syrup than any other ingredient. (Yes, you're probably going to want to return that product to the store shelf!)

Nutrition Facts

Serving Size 1 cup (30 g)
Servings Per Container About 10

Amount Per Serving

Calories 110   Calories from Fat 10

	% Daily Value*
Total Fat 1 g	2%
Saturated Fat 0 g	0%
Cholesterol	0%
Sodium	10%
Total Carbohydrate	8%
Dietary Fiber 3 g	10%
Sugars 6 g	
Protein 3 g	

Vitamin A 25% • Vitamin C 25%
Calcium 4% • Iron 45%

* Percent Daily Values are based on a 2,000 calorie diet. Your daily values might be higher or lower depending on your calorie needs:

		Calories:	2,000	2,500
Total Fat	Less than		65 g	80 g
Sat Fat	Less than		20 g	25 g
Cholesterol	Less than		300 mg	300 mg
Sodium	Less than		2,400 mg	2,400 mg
Total Carbohydrate			300 g	375 g
Dietary Fiber			25 g	30 g

Calories per gram:
Fat 9 • Carbohydrate 4 • Protein 4

100% whole-wheat bread. With a little practice, you and your children can easily and quickly make smart food choices.

6. HAVE REGULAR HOME FAMILY MEALS. It may seem impossible to reorganize your schedule to allow one unrushed meal a day together, but this can have an enormous effect on your child's health and happiness. Your children need all the support they can get to learn about healthy eating. And your children learn best about nutrition while eating with their family and from the examples you set. Regular family meals can also contribute to children's emotional well-being. Whether your family is a single-parent household with one child or a two-parent household with a brood of twelve, if you have a place to live and a table where you eat, you have what you need to get started.

OVERWEIGHT CHILDREN: OUR KIDS IN CRISIS

There's not much doubt about it: Childhood obesity in America is an epidemic. One child in five is overweight, and the number of overweight children has doubled in the last three decades. In California, more than 25% of children are overweight—and nearly 40% are physically unfit.

Overweight kids now face serious diseases such as type 2 diabetes, which once occurred primarily in adults with poor eating and exercise habits. And anyone who carried a few extra pounds as a child has a pretty good idea of the social problems an overweight child faces.

Health problems facing overweight children include:

- Type 2 diabetes, often caused by obesity and poor eating habits (previously called adult-onset diabetes).

- High cholesterol and blood pressure levels, which are risk factors for heart disease.

- Sleep apnea (interrupted breathing while sleeping), which may lead to problems with learning and memory.

- Increased incidence of orthopedic problems, liver disease, and asthma.

- A 70% chance of becoming overweight or obese adults.

And, perhaps most importantly, you need to lead by example. You are your children's most influential teachers. "Do as I say, not as I do," will not work when trying to get your kids to eat healthier. So be prepared to do everything you encourage your child to do—which includes following the six keys to healthy eating yourself.

That's it! *That's what a parent should do!*

Exercise with your child, help your child to develop a positive body image, and practice these keys to healthy eating—and you will be building into your children the defenses they need to live in a health-hostile world.

CHAPTER 2

How to Make It All Work

Changing eating habits can be difficult, and it is even more difficult to do it alone. So for anyone who wants to eat healthily, have more energy, and lose weight, this is a great place to start.

Sitting Down at the Family Table

Sure, your life is hectic, and sure, everyone has meetings and games and events to rush off to. And of course it seems faster and easier to zap some Hot Pockets in the microwave to eat on the way out the door, or grab fast-food burgers while running errands.

As we mentioned in the last chapter, at KidShape we've found that one of the most important things you can do toward setting your family on a path to lasting health and good eating habits is to eat together as a family. Of course, you're not going to be able to do it every meal—and perhaps not every evening. But you can carve out some time and set a schedule to ensure that you, as a family, sit down to a meal where you can not only bond as a family but develop solid nutritional habits that will stay with you and your children for life. It's a wonderful gift to give your children—and yourself. Little League may be important, but forming good eating habits is a gift for life.

If you have a table or a countertop where you can gather, you have what you need to get started. You can prepare a meal ahead of time and pull it out of the freezer, or you can simmer a hearty stew all day in a slow cooker and serve it in the evening. At the family table, you're not only reinforcing good habits, but establishing a warm and calm environment where you can enjoy a meal while your children have a chance to get your full attention and to know they are being listened to and included in your life.

Our Recipes

KidShape Café features recipes your children will love, including healthy versions of favorites such as burgers and fries, macaroni and cheese, and brownies. Most of the recipes were developed by David Lawrence, a personal chef and cookbook author, and have been kid-tested and approved by children David has cooked for. The book also includes some recipes we have used in the KidShape program that have been proven effective and delicious. All these recipes are healthy without compromising taste—your kids certainly won't feel deprived eating these foods! Your children will enjoy eating them as much as we do.

We've included tasty and healthier versions of many of your old favorites—which we have labeled as Kids' Classics—as well as some that may introduce you to new tastes. They reflect the multicultural, wide-ranging tastes we see in Southern California, modified to suit a healthy lifestyle. We have been careful to limit amounts of sugar and fat—but at the same time keep these foods tasty enough for even a finicky eater.

You'll see that we have included a nutritional analysis of each recipe, listing calories and grams of fat, protein, and carbohydrates, along with the number of exchange or portions from each food group. For instance, our English Muffin French Toast has 205 calories with 10 grams of protein, 40 grams of carbohydrates, and 2 grams of fat—which works out to 2 food group servings of grain, 1/4 serving of milk/yogurt, and 1/2 serving each of protein and fat.

How do you know what's right for your child? Your pediatrician may have supplied you an eating plan. If not, refer to our "Calorie Needs" chart on page 13, which gives basic calorie levels and food group servings for various age groups.

CALORIE NEEDS

	Overweight children, ages 5–8	Overweight children, ages 9–11	Adult women and anyone above age 70	Overweight children, ages 12–14	Adult men	Teen girls and athletic women	Teen boys and athletic men
Calorie level	About 1,300	About 1,500	1,600–1,800	About 1,800	2,000–2,400	2,000–2,200	2,800–3,000
Grain servings	4	5	6	8	9	9	11
Vegetable servings	3	3	3	3	4	4	5
Fruit group servings	2	2	2	4	4	3	4
Milk /yogurt servings	2	2	2 to 3	3	3	2 to 3	2 to 3
Lean protein servings	4 ounces	4 ounces	5 ounces	6 ounces	6 ounces	6 ounces	7 ounces
Total fat	40 grams	46 grams	53 grams	60 grams	67 grams	73 grams	93 grams

Never Single Out a Family Member

Perhaps only one of your children is overweight. If you've tried serving that child smaller portions or denying her dessert, you probably already know that doesn't work. It results in a child who is embarrassed, frustrated, or resentful—or all three! This child will likely stop at the local convenience store and buy a Milky Way or two on her way to school, or cadge a frosted cupcake from a friend's lunch.

Your entire family should eat the same foods. A tasty and healthy meal, with correct portion sizes, is suitable for everyone.

A child generally becomes overweight in response to poor eating and exercise habits, and usually those are family-wide habits. You can't expect your child to snack on celery and carrot sticks while you're digging into a bag of Doritos. (Realize also that a child may be overeating in response to family or school pressures, and you'll need to delve into those.) Clear out unhealthy and unnutritious foods from your home—and stick to the healthy eating habits you want your children to follow.

This means you'll all be eating the same foods—in varying amounts, of course, according to each family member's energy needs.

Determining Portion Sizes

This exercise will help you and your children determine appropriate serving sizes. You'll need measuring cups, measuring spoons, and a food scale, and the plates and bowls you commonly use.

Go to your cupboards or refrigerator and find 10 different food items, including liquids. Include foods such as cereals, bread, milk, juice, meat, sugar, ketchup, and a fat such as butter.

Set out the amount of food you normally eat in one sitting. For instance, fill a cereal bowl as you normally would. Try to guess how much this is in cups. Then look at the label for your cereal, and see how much is supposed to be in one serving. Use a measuring cup and measure that amount and place it in another bowl. Compare it to the bowl you've already poured. Have you been eating more than one serving?

Do this for each of the foods you've taken out. Let your children practice pouring out specific amounts so they will become accustomed to these measurements. You and your children will quickly become familiar with what a serving size looks like in your dishes, and won't have to continue measuring foods.

Here are single-serving sizes of common foods according to food groups.

GRAIN (Bread, Cereal, Rice, Pasta, Starchy Vegetable)

There are two types of grains, whole grains and refined or processed grains. Whole grains are healthier because they have more fiber and more nutrients, and are also more filling. At least half of the grain foods you and your children eat should be from the whole grain group. One grain serving (or a one-ounce equivalent) equals the following:

WHOLE GRAINS

1 slice of whole-wheat bread
½ whole-wheat hot dog or hamburger bun
½ whole-wheat English muffin

½ cup brown rice

5 whole-wheat crackers

3 cups popcorn

½ cup cooked oatmeal

1 cup whole-grain cold cereal, such as whole-wheat cereal flakes or muesli

REFINED GRAINS/STARCHY VEGETABLES

1 slice of bread

½ bagel, English muffin, hamburger or hot dog bun

6-inch pita bread

¾ cup unsweetened dry cereal or ½ cup sugar-frosted cereal

½ cup cooked cereal, rice, or pasta

5 or 6 small crackers, low-fat or nonfat

½ cup corn, green peas, mashed potatoes, yams, or sweet potatoes

1 cup winter squash

1 small baked or broiled potato

3 cups popcorn

1 corn tortilla, 6 inches

1 flour tortilla, 8 inches

1 waffle, 4½ inches square, reduced fat

VEGETABLE (Nonstarchy)

1 cup raw vegetables

½ cup cooked vegetables (excluding corn, peas, potatoes, winter squash)

½ cup vegetable juice

½ cup tomato sauce

FRUIT

1 small fresh fruit

½ cup fruit juice

¼ cup dried fruit

1 frozen 100% fruit juice bar

½ cup fruit, canned (not in heavy syrup)

MILK/YOGURT

1 cup skim, $\frac{1}{2}$%, or 1% fat milk, or nonfat or low-fat buttermilk

$\frac{1}{2}$ cup nonfat dry milk or $\frac{1}{2}$ cup evaporated skim milk

1 cup nonfat or low-fat flavored or plain yogurt

PROTEIN

Lean Protein (1 ounce)

1 ounce lean poultry, beef, pork, lamb, game, shellfish, or fish with no skin and all
   excess fat cut off

1 ounce low-fat or nonfat cheese or deli meat (3 grams or less fat per ounce)

$\frac{1}{2}$ cup cooked dried beans, lentils, or other legumes

2 egg whites

$\frac{1}{4}$ cup nonfat or low-fat cottage cheese

1 lean turkey hot dog (3 grams fat or less per ounce)

Medium-Fat Protein (1 ounce protein + 1 fat serving)

1 cup soy milk

1 ounce fried chicken

1 ounce feta or mozzarella cheese

$\frac{1}{4}$ cup ricotta cheese

High-Fat Protein (1 ounce protein + 2 fat servings)

1 ounce cheese

1 ounce processed sandwich meat, such as bologna or salami

2 tablespoons natural peanut butter

10 peanuts or 6 mixed nuts, almonds, or cashews, or 4 pecan or walnut halves

1 regular hot dog, beef or pork

FATS/SWEETS (45 calories)

1 teaspoon regular or 1 tablespoon reduced-fat oil, margarine, butter, or mayonnaise

1 tablespoon salad dressing or 2 tablespoons reduced-fat salad dressing

1 tablespoon cream cheese or 2 tablespoons reduced-fat cream cheese

$\frac{1}{8}$ avocado

$\frac{1}{2}$ cup light or reduced-fat ice cream or $\frac{1}{4}$ cup ice cream

2 teaspoons tahini paste

1 teaspoon lard or shortening

2 tablespoons chitterlings, boiled

2 small cookies

½ frosted cupcake

½ sweet roll or pan dulce

Grocery Shopping Strategies

Obviously you can't prepare healthy meals if you don't have the ingredients you need. What's necessary is some advance planning so that your freezer, fridge, and pantry are well stocked—with something always on hand to make a nutritious meal.

Eventually healthy shopping will become second nature and you won't even have to think about filling your shopping cart. In the meantime, here are a few ways to simplify your shopping task.

- Make a list and stick to it. Staying focused will help you avoid impulse buying.
- Never go to the store hungry! Your defenses will be down and you'll suddenly find yourself with a cart full of high-calorie foods you don't need.
- Shop the perimeter of the store first, where you'll find whole foods such as produce and meats, then head for the freezer section. You may want to skip certain aisles altogether.
- Read food labels to help you make the most nutritious selections.
- Involve the kids. Unless they're toddlers or younger (in which case you may want to swap off childcare so you can zoom through your shopping), children can be a big help in the grocery store. Give them "assignments" ahead of time— you can have one child select apples and another find the whole-wheat pasta.
- Avoid the candy aisle and be prepared for the cereal and frozen dessert sections by having choices already marked on your list. Let your child locate the Cheerios and 100% frozen juice bars and place them in the cart.
- Consider making a master shopping list, organized the way your store is laid out, to use each week.
- Stay firm and committed to your goal of healthy eating.

Stocking a Healthy Kitchen

Let's face it—trying to feed your family nutritious and healthy meals while juggling sports, homework, and ballet lessons can be challenging at best. One of the best tools is a well-stocked kitchen. It's much easier to make wise choices when you set yourself up for success. With a few basics on hand, you'll not only be able to make wiser choices in the kitchen, but you'll be able to think on your feet, make fewer trips to the market, and increase the variety of your meals.

If you're just getting started, here are the basics for your refrigerator and pantry.

Fresh and frozen vegetables
Fresh and juice-packed fruits
Whole-grain breads and tortillas
Whole-grain cereals and oatmeal
Whole-wheat pasta and yolkless noodles
Chicken breasts
Ground white-meat turkey
Water-packed tuna
Nonfat yogurt and milk
Low-fat cheese
Natural peanut butter; all-fruit jelly
Egg substitute
Plain cereal, such as old-fashioned oatmeal, bran flakes, or Cheerios

More time to shop? Consider adding these items to your shopping list. (You'll find recipes that use them in the pages ahead.)

YOUR PANTRY

MISCELLANEOUS

Flour
Cocoa powder
Cornstarch
Low-sodium chicken stock
Low-sodium beef stock

Low-sodium vegetable stock
Water-packed artichokes
Canned tomatoes: crushed,
    diced, and whole
Sun-dried tomatoes

Sugar-free applesauce
Raisins
Prunes
Evaporated skim milk
Dried bread crumbs (seasoned and
   unseasoned)

DRIED PASTAS AND RICE
Bow ties, angel hair, spaghetti, lasagna,
   shells, elbows

Varieties of rice including Arborio,
   basmati, brown, long grain, wild

CANNED BEANS
Black beans
Kidney beans
Chick-peas
Vegetarian refried beans

SURVIVING THE FAST-FOOD RESTAURANT

Of course eating at home or munching on a home-packed lunch is healthier than dining at a fast-food establishment, but sometimes you just can't avoid it. Your son's soccer team may stop there after a game or your daughter may be visiting her best friend and her family wants to go—so you and your kids need to know the best choices to make in these situations.

Here are some fast-food survival tips.

- Ask the server to leave off the mayonnaise and dressings such as "special sauce"—these add lots of calories and fat.

- Choose milk or water instead of soda.

- Order a side salad and use dressing lightly. Avoid toppings such as bacon bits and olives.

- Order small fries instead of large, or a plain baked potato instead of fries.

- Ask for fruit wedges instead of fries in children's meals—and use lightly (or avoid entirely) that sweet "dipping sauce" for fruit.

- Choose grilled or baked meats, not fried.

- Skip the burger entirely and order chili or a salad instead.

- Choose veggie or cheese pizza rather than ones with meat.

- Opt for small portions—often you'll find these on the "dollar" menu.

BREADS

Whole-wheat English muffins

Whole-wheat pita bread

Whole-grain bread

Low-fat, whole-wheat tortillas

Corn tortillas

CEREALS

Whole-grain cereals

Rolled oats/oatmeal

Bran-flaked cereals

CONDIMENTS

Mustards

Ketchup

Honey

Salsa

Pickles

Chutney

Light Worcestershire sauce

Light soy sauce

Hoisin sauce

Tomato sauce and tomato paste

All-fruit jelly

Light maple syrup

Fat-free and reduced-fat salad dressings

Natural peanut butter

Vinegar: balsamic, red wine, white wine,
    cider, rice

DRIED HERBS/SPICES

Cracked black pepper

Basil

Bay leaves

Cardamom

Cayenne pepper

Chili powder

Chives

Cinnamon

Cloves

Coriander

Crushed red pepper flakes

Cumin

Curry powder

Dill

Extracts: vanilla, almond

Garlic powder

Italian herb seasoning

Kosher salt

Marjoram

Nutmeg

Oregano

Paprika

Parsley

Rosemary

Hot pepper sauce

Tarragon

Thyme

YOUR FREEZER

Corn

Green peas

Broccoli

Carrots

Cauliflower

Spinach

Berries, mangoes, and peaches

Skinless chicken breasts

Ground turkey breast

Seafood, such as fresh cod, flounder, snapper, salmon, shrimp, and crab

YOUR REFRIGERATOR

Egg substitute

Nonfat milk

Nonfat yogurt

Nonfat cottage cheese

Nonfat sour cream

FRESH FRUIT

Apples

Berries

Melons

Oranges

Peaches

FRESH VEGETABLES

Asparagus

Bell peppers, green, red, and yellow

Broccoli

Carrots

Cauliflower

Celery

Mushrooms

Onions, red and yellow

Spinach

Squash

Zucchini

FRESH HERBS

Basil

Thyme

Tarragon

Cilantro

Parsley

Garlic

Gingerroot

Modifying Your Own Recipes

While we've supplied delicious recipes in this book, you may have favorites that you'd like to modify so they're healthier. Here are a few ways to alter your own recipes.

Instead of	Change to	Benefit	Approximate calories saved
Fats and Sweets			
Oil (in dressings)	Water	Less fat	180
Oil or butter to sauté	Nonstick skillet	Less fat	125 per tablespoon
Sauté in butter	Sauté in broth	Less fat and cholesterol	104 per tablespoon

continued on next page

Instead of	Change to	Benefit	Approximate calories saved
Fats and Sweets *cont.*			
2/3 cup mayonnaise	1/3 cup mayonnaise and 1/3 cup nonfat yogurt	Less fat	480
Mayonnaise	Mustard or low-fat mayonnaise	Less fat	95 per tablespoon
Butter or syrup on pancakes, waffles, French toast	Pureed berries	Less fat and less refined sugar	90 per teaspoon butter 40 per teaspoon syrup
Oil dressing on pasta salad	Reduce amount of dressing by 1/4 cup	Less fat	600
Mayonnaise in dressing	Yogurt in dressing	Less fat	480 per 1/3 cup
Mayonnaise in dressing	Buttermilk in dressing	Less fat	500 per 1/3 cup
Cream	Plain nonfat yogurt	Less fat	720 per cup
Sour cream	Plain nonfat yogurt or nonfat sour cream	Less fat	360 per cup
Milk			
1/3 cup evaporated milk	1/3 cup skim evaporated milk	Less fat	50
Whole milk	Nonfat milk	Less fat	60 per cup
1/2 cup whole milk	1/2 cup nonfat milk	Less fat	30
Protein			
4 eggs	1 egg and 2 egg whites 3/4 cup applesauce	Less fat and cholesterol	193
Chicken with skin	Chicken without skin	Less fat	360
2/3 cup cheese	1/3 cup part-skim cheese	Less fat	100
Oil-packed tuna	Water-packed tuna	Less fat	220
Tuna with 5 tablespoons mayonnaise	Tuna with 3 tablespoons mayonnaise	Less fat	200
Chili with 1 pound ground beef	Chili with 1/2 pound ground beef	Less fat	400
Untrimmed steak	Trimmed steak	Less fat	55 per ounce
Buttered salted popcorn	Plain popcorn	Less fat and sodium	20 per cup

Instead of	Change to	Benefit	Approximate calories saved
Protein *cont.*			
Full-fat cheese	Part-skim cheese	Less fat	10–25 per ounce
Bologna	Sliced chicken	Less fat	40 per ounce
Ground beef in tacos	Diced chicken in tacos	Less fat	300 per pound
Fruit			
Grapefruit juice, 8 ounces	½ grapefruit	Less sugar and more fiber	60
Grains			
Tortillas, fried	Baked	Less fat	45 per tortilla

DRINK, DRINK, DRINK

One of the first things you'll want to do to improve your family's health is to cut out sodas—your children may whine for them, but stay firm. Sodas are filled with empty calories, and many of them have caffeine as well—not what your child needs. In the last 30 years the amount of soft drinks consumed by children has doubled. Today you can buy a 64-ounce "super size" soft drink—that's half a gallon!

Soft drinks are high in sugar but contain no nutritional value. And caffeine is a stimulant that increases the heart rate and heart contractions, potentially causing tremors, anxiety, and insomnia. But soft drinks are also packed with phosphoric acid, which weakens the bones by promoting the loss of calcium and demineralizes teeth, contributing to tooth decay.

You also need to limit juice. Yes, you read that right. Sure, juices have some vitamins, but they're also loaded with calories and sugar—it's natural sugar, but still sugar. Apple juice, in particular, is little more than sugar and water. If your child asks for juice, offer a piece of fruit instead—it's much healthier, packed with fiber and nutrients, and contains far fewer calories. Limit your children's juice to one 4-ounce serving a day. If you can dilute the juice with water, better yet.

Sports drinks are also filled with sugar. A sports drink is needed (to help replace electrolytes) only if you exercise steadily for more than an hour. Again, you may want to dilute them with water.

But the human body does need liquid. Every chemical reaction that goes on inside your body requires it, and water is how your body gets rid of the toxins that build up in your cells. Without enough water, you can become dehydrated, which can cause headaches, a tired and groggy feeling, and dry skin—and sometimes when you think you're hungry, what you actually need is fluid.

Get in the habit of serving only water and low-fat or nonfat milk with meals (children younger than two should have whole milk, not reduced fat). Children need calcium and vitamin D to help build strong bones and teeth, and milk is an easy way to deliver it. (Consult your pediatrician if your child appears to have trouble tolerating milk, or try lactose-reduced milks.)

Generally, active adults age 16 and older should drink eight 8-ounce glasses of water a day, and children 6 and older should drink six 8-ounce glasses of water. Flavor water with lemon or a sprig of mint if desired. Having their own colorful water bottle can help children with this new water-drinking habit.

CHAPTER 3

Breakfast and Breads

Are your kids in the habit of grabbing a sweet roll or gobbling a bowl of sugary cereal in the morning? This just isn't enough fuel to get them through the day—and a child who starts off the day without a nutritious breakfast will likely be craving more sweet foods as soon as the sugar wears off.

Or perhaps your kids rush out the door without breakfast. Kids have more energy and do better in school when they eat breakfast, and kids who skip breakfast are more likely to be overweight.

Instead, start your child's day with a hearty Breakfast Pizza, Egg 'n' Ham Breakfast Sandwich, or Pumpkin Pancakes—or any of these selections. (Never fear, you can prepare many of these ahead of time.) And set a good example for your child—be sure you take time to eat breakfast!

QUICK 'N' EASY BREAKFASTS

No time to prepare breakfast? Or perhaps your kids insist on doing it themselves.

Here are some simple breakfasts that take only a few minutes, which your kids can prepare on their own. Your children will have a sense of satisfaction at having made their own meal—and you'll have a sense of relief that they're starting the day with a healthy breakfast.

Quick breakfast 1:

▲ ¾ cup Cheerios or whole-grain cereal

▲ 8 ounces nonfat milk

▲ Fruit (½ banana, 1 cup berries or melon, or 1 orange)

Quick breakfast 2:

▲ Old-fashioned oatmeal (cook for three minutes in the microwave—in a large bowl so it doesn't boil over)

▲ ¼ cup raisins

▲ 1 teaspoon honey

▲ 8 ounces nonfat milk

Quick breakfast 3:

▲ 1 Eggo whole-wheat frozen waffle

▲ 1 tablespoon peanut butter

▲ Fruit (½ banana, 1 cup berries or melon, or 1 orange)

Other quick 'n' easy choices might include a peanut butter and jelly sandwich and a glass of nonfat milk, cottage cheese and fruit, a bagel with low-fat cream cheese and an apple, or yogurt mixed with whole-grain cereal. Even an energy bar eaten on the way to the bus stop is better than no breakfast!

EGG 'N' HAM BREAKFAST SANDWICH

(Makes 4 servings)

322 calories
Protein 25 g
Carbohydrate 29 g
Fat 11 g

Food group servings:
Grain 2
Milk/Yogurt 0.1
Protein 3.4
Fat 2.2

This is "fast food" you can feel good about giving your kids in the morning—it's low fat as well as delicious. Wrap this sandwich in a paper towel and kids can eat it on the run. It's truly portable food.

Nonstick cooking spray
1 cup egg substitute, such as Egg Beaters
¼ cup nonfat milk
¼ teaspoon salt
⅛ teaspoon black pepper

½ cup chopped cooked ham
4 English muffins, halved and toasted
4 slices low-fat American cheese, halved

Preheat the broiler.

Spray a medium skillet with nonstick spray and heat over medium heat. In a small bowl, beat together egg substitute, milk, salt, and pepper. Pour the egg mixture into the skillet and sprinkle the ham on top. Cook without stirring until the mixture begins to set on the bottom and around the egg. Using a heat-proof rubber spatula, push the edges in slightly to allow the uncooked portion to flow underneath. Continue cooking until cooked through but still glossy on top. Remove from heat.

Place English muffin halves on a baking sheet and top each with a slice of cheese and one-fourth of the egg mixture. Top with remaining cheese slices. Broil 4 to 5 inches from the heat for 1 minute or until the cheese melts. Top with remaining muffin halves. Serve immediately.

ABOUT EGG SUBSTITUTES

You'll almost always find egg substitute in the refrigerated egg case next to whole eggs. The name brand is Egg Beaters, and you may find generic or store brands that are a few cents cheaper. Essentially these are egg whites, colored by beta carotene, with a few added nutrients. They have no fat or cholesterol, and less than half the calories of a regular egg. They work in any recipe that calls for eggs ($\frac{1}{4}$ cup = 1 egg) and can be scrambled, made into omelets, and so on.

You'll also find varieties, such as Southwestern, that make great omelets. Egg substitute is also great in any recipe that calls for raw egg yolk (such as Caesar salad dressing). Because it's pasteurized, you don't have to worry about the health risk of eating raw egg.

205 calories
Protein 10 g
Carbohydrate 40 g
Fat 3 g

Food group servings:
Grain 2
Milk/Yogurt 0.25
Protein 0.5
Fat 0.5

ENGLISH MUFFIN FRENCH TOAST

(Makes 4 servings)

This is a fun twist on conventional French toast. Your kids will like the fun shape and crunch of the English muffins, and you'll like how easy this recipe is to prepare.

¼	cup egg substitute		Butter-flavored nonstick
2	egg whites		cooking spray
1	cup nonfat milk	2	tablespoons liquid Butter Buds
¼	teaspoon ground cinnamon	4	tablespoons reduced-calorie
4	English muffins		maple syrup, heated

Preheat the oven to 200°.

Whisk the egg substitute and egg whites, milk, and cinnamon in a shallow dish. Split the English muffins and place split side down in milk mixture for 4 minutes. Turn and soak for 1 minute more. Spray a nonstick skillet with butter-flavored cooking spray and place the English muffins in the pan, cut side down. Cook for about 3 minutes on moderate heat, until browned. Turn and brown the other side, about 3 minutes more (respray the pan as needed). Keep warm in preheated oven while continuing to cook remaining muffins. Serve with Butter Buds and warm syrup.

FRENCH TOAST
(Makes 5 servings)

582 calories
Protein 10 g
Carbohydrate 31 g
Fat 6 g

Food group servings:
Grain 2
Milk/Yogurt 0.1
Protein 1
Fat 1.2

It's absolutely true! You can have French toast and you can make it low fat with just a few simple modifications. If this doesn't get your kids out of bed in the morning, nothing will.

1 **cup egg substitute**	**Butter-flavored nonstick**
⅓ **cup nonfat milk**	**cooking spray**
1 **teaspoon ground cinnamon**	10 **slices nonfat white bread**
1 **teaspoon vanilla extract**	5 **tablespoons reduced-calorie**
	maple syrup

In a shallow pie dish combine the egg substitute, milk, cinnamon, and vanilla. Spray a large nonstick skillet with butter-flavored cooking spray, and heat over medium heat. Dip both sides of the bread slices in the egg mixture and brown for about 3 minutes on each side. Respray the pan as needed. Serve immediately with the syrup.

Calories 262
Protein 12 g
Carbohydrate 36 g
Fat 10 g

Food group servings:
Grain 2.4
Vegetable 0.2
Protein 1
Fat 2

BREAKFAST PIZZA

(Makes 8 servings)

Every kid loves pizza for breakfast. But instead of serving high-fat leftovers, why not make this delicious, healthy breakfast pizza? With a little fore-thought—simply placing the hash browns in the fridge the night before to thaw and spending a few minutes chopping the vegetables—you can have this hearty breakfast on the table in about 15 minutes on a busy morning. Or prepare it the night before so it's ready to pop in the oven.

Nonstick cooking spray	¼ cup nonfat milk
1½ cups frozen diced or shredded hash brown potatoes, thawed	1 tablespoon chopped fresh cilantro
¼ cup sliced green onions	1 (16-ounce) prepared pizza crust
¼ cup diced green bell pepper	½ cup grated low-fat Monterey Jack cheese
¼ teaspoon ground cumin	1 small tomato, seeded and chopped
1 garlic clove, minced	
1 cup egg substitute	

Preheat the oven to 375°.

Spray a large nonstick skillet with nonstick cooking spray and place over medium heat. Add the potatoes, green onion, bell pepper, cumin, and garlic. Cook until the vegetables are tender, about 3 minutes.

Meanwhile, in a small bowl, beat together the egg substitute, milk, and cilantro. Add to the potato mixture in the skillet and cook without stirring, until the mixture begins to set on the bottom and around the edge. Using a heat-proof rubber spatula, push the edges in slightly to allow the uncooked portion to flow underneath. Continue cooking until cooked through but still glossy on top. Remove from heat.

To assemble pizza, place the pizza crust on a baking sheet and sprinkle with half of the cheese. Place the egg mixture on top and sprinkle with the remaining cheese and the chopped tomato. Bake for 8 to 10 minutes, or until cheese is melted. Slice into 8 wedges and serve immediately.

PUMPKIN PANCAKES

(Makes 8 servings, 2 pancakes per serving)

These pancakes are like pumpkin pie for breakfast. What kid (or adult) could resist?

Calories 181
Protein 7 g
Carbohydrate 40 g
Fat 2 g

Food group servings:
Grain 1.5
Milk/Yogurt 0.2
Protein 0.1
Fat 0.4

2	cups all-purpose flour	1	cup canned pumpkin puree
2	tablespoons packed brown sugar	½	cup egg substitute
1	tablespoon baking powder	2	tablespoons liquid Butter Buds Nonstick cooking spray
½	teaspoon salt	8	tablespoons reduced-calorie maple syrup
½	teaspoon pumpkin pie spice		
1½	cups nonfat milk		

Preheat the oven to 200°.

In a medium bowl whisk together the flour, brown sugar, baking powder, salt, and pumpkin pie spice.

In another medium bowl combine the milk, pumpkin puree, egg substitute, and the liquid Butter Buds. Add the wet ingredients to the dry all at once and stir just until moistened. The batter will be lumpy.

Lightly coat a nonstick griddle or skillet with nonstick cooking spray and place over medium heat. For each pancake pour ¼ cup of the batter onto the hot skillet and cook about 2 minutes on each side until small bubbles form and break on the top and the edges look slightly dry. Turn and cook the other side until brown. Keep warm in a preheated oven and serve warm with syrup.

BUTTER BUDS, SMART BALANCE, AND YOU

Fats and oils, consumed in moderation, can be a part of a healthy diet. They become a problem, however, when we eat too much, especially too much saturated fats, trans fats, and cholesterol.

Reading labels becomes extremely useful, because they list not only the total amount of fat but the types of fat. Most fats should come from polyunsaturated and monounsaturated fat, like the fat found in some fish, nuts, and vegetable oils.

You'll notice that many of our recipes use Butter Buds instead of butter, margarine, or oil. You can buy them in granule form (called Sprinkles) or in Butter Buds Mix, which you mix with water to form a liquid.

Butter Buds is free of fat and cholesterol, with 15 calories per tablespoon. (Butter or margarine has about 100 calories and 12 grams of fat per tablespoon.)

Butter Buds contain maltodextrin, a carbohydrate from corn; flavoring from butter oils; salt; dehydrated butter; guar gum; and baking soda.

Frying or sautéing in Butter Buds is not recommended, however. You can sauté in broth; a small amount of olive oil (120 calories per tablespoon); or a product such as Smart Balance, a vegetable oil blend with no hydrogenation, no cholesterol, and no trans-fatty acids. Smart Balance Buttery Spread or bottled oil is 80 calories per tablespoon and can be used for cooking and pan-frying; Smart Balance Light Buttery Spread is 45 calories per tablespoon and suitable for light sautéing or broiling. Both of these products can be used as a spread, like butter.

WHOLE-WHEAT BLUEBERRY PANCAKES

(Makes 10 servings, 2 pancakes per serving)

Serve these pancakes and your kids will think you're a hero.

Calories 186
Protein 8 g
Carbohydrate 36 g
Fat 3 g

Food group servings:
Grain 1.5
Milk/Yogurt 0.2
Fruit 0.2
Protein 0.1
Fat 0.6

1¼ cups whole-wheat flour	2 tablespoons liquid Butter Buds
1¼ cups all-purpose flour	1 cup fresh or frozen blueberries, thawed
2 tablespoons baking powder	
2 tablespoons sugar	Nonstick cooking spray
1 cup egg substitute	10 tablespoons reduced-calorie maple syrup
1¾ cups nonfat milk	

Preheat the oven to 200°.

In a medium bowl whisk together the two types of flour, baking powder, and sugar.

In another medium bowl combine the egg substitute, milk, and liquid Butter Buds. Add the wet ingredients to the dry all at once and stir just until moistened. The batter will be lumpy. Fold in the blueberries.

Lightly coat a nonstick griddle or skillet with nonstick cooking spray and place over medium heat. For each pancake pour ¼ cup of the batter onto the hot skillet and cook about 2 minutes or until bubbles form and break on top and edges look dry. Turn and cook the other side. Keep warm in a preheated oven and serve warm with syrup.

ZUCCHINI BREAD

(Makes 2 loaves; 24 servings, 12 servings per loaf)

Trust me, they won't even know the zucchini is in there. Just don't tell your kids the name of this recipe until they're on their second slice.

	Nonstick cooking spray	¾	cup egg substitute
3	cups all-purpose flour	1	cup liquid Butter Buds
1	tablespoon ground cinnamon	2	teaspoons vanilla extract
1	teaspoon salt	1	cup sugar
1	teaspoon baking soda	1	cup brown sugar
1	teaspoon baking powder	2	cups shredded zucchini

Preheat the oven to 350°.

Spray two 9 x 5-inch loaf pans with nonstick cooking spray and set aside. In a medium bowl whisk together the flour, cinnamon, salt, baking soda, and baking powder, and set aside. In a large bowl mix together the egg substitute, Butter Buds, and vanilla. Stir in the sugars and the other dry ingredients. Fold in the shredded zucchini and pour the batter into the prepared loaf pans. Bake for 60 to 70 minutes, until a toothpick inserted in the middle comes out clean. Cool in the pans 2 minutes, then remove and cool completely.

Calories 135
Protein 3 g
Carbohydrate 30 g
Fat 1 g

Food group servings:
Grain 0.5
Vegetable 0.5
Fat 0.2

BANANA BREAD

(Makes 1 loaf; 12 servings)

There is nothing quite like a slice of warm, moist banana bread just out of the oven. This is just like grandma's recipe—with a few modifications, of course. You can serve it with peanut butter, spread lightly, and a glass of milk.

Nonstick cooking spray	¼ cup oat bran
1¾ cups all-purpose flour	½ cup egg substitute
2 teaspoons baking powder	1 cup lightly packed brown sugar
½ teaspoon ground cinnamon	⅓ cup liquid Butter Buds
¼ teaspoon ground cloves	3 medium, ripe bananas, mashed
¼ teaspoon salt	

Preheat the oven to 350°.

Spray a 9 x 5-inch loaf pan with nonstick cooking spray and set aside. In a large bowl, whisk together the flour, baking powder, cinnamon, cloves, and salt. Stir in the oat bran and set aside. In a small bowl, beat together the egg substitute, brown sugar, and liquid Butter Buds. Fold in the bananas. Add the wet ingredients to the dry and mix just until combined. Pour into the prepared loaf pan and bake for 50 minutes. Cool in the pan 2 minutes, then remove from pan and cool completely.

PUMPKIN BREAD

(Makes 3 loaves; 36 servings, 12 servings per loaf)

This bread is amazing warm out of the oven, or as toast the next day. It's all the flavors of pumpkin pie in bread form. (You can pop extra loaves in the freezer.)

Nonstick cooking spray	1 teaspoon ground cinnamon
1 cup liquid Butter Buds	1 teaspoon salt
1½ cups Splenda Sugar Blend for Baking	1 (16-ounce) can pumpkin puree
1 cup egg substitute	⅔ cup water
1 teaspoon nutmeg	2 teaspoons baking soda
	3 cups all-purpose flour

Preheat the oven to 350°.

Spray three 9 x 5-inch loaf pans with nonstick cooking spray and set aside. In a large bowl beat together the Butter Buds, Splenda, egg substitute, nutmeg, cinnamon, salt, and pumpkin puree until smooth. Add the water, baking soda, and flour and stir to blend. Pour the batter into the prepared loaf pans and bake for 45 to 55 minutes until a toothpick inserted in the middle comes out clean. Cool for 2 minutes in the pans, then remove and cool completely.

ENERGY BARS

The granola bar has evolved into many new types of bars, including cereal bars and energy bars. Today you can find a variety of energy bars in almost every grocery store and often even in convenience stores and gas stations. You can even find special formulations for men, women, athletes, and the elderly.

Energy bars have a variety of advantages over the traditional granola bar and cereal bar. Typically energy bars have extra protein and are fortified with multiple vitamins and minerals. Of course a real meal is best, but energy bars can be a healthy alternative to skipping meals or snacks, especially breakfast. Teens frequently skip breakfast and lunch for a variety of reasons, including not waking up early enough to eat breakfast, feeling that it is not "cool" to bring a lunch from home even though they don't like cafeteria food, or being embarrassed to eat in front of their friends, especially if they are overweight.

Energy bars are a quick and easy way for teens to eat something instead of skipping meals—and far better for them than candy bars.

HAWAIIAN SWEET BREAD

(Makes 2 loaves; 24 servings, 12 servings per loaf)

I love this slightly sweet (and wonderfully low-fat) bread right out of the oven. But I really love it as toast in the morning. It does take a while to prepare, but it's more than worth it! It makes two loaves, so you can pop one in the freezer for later.

1	large baking potato	½	cup liquid Butter Buds
¾	cup sugar, plus 3 tablespoons	1	cup egg substitute, divided
1	package dry yeast	4	cups all-purpose flour
⅓	cup nonfat milk		Nonstick cooking spray
1¼	teaspoons salt		

Boil the potato until soft. Save ⅓ cup of the boiling water and cool to lukewarm. Peel and mash the potato and measure out ½ cup. Add 3 tablespoons of the sugar and yeast to the lukewarm water and stir to dissolve. Stir in the potato mixture and set aside to rise until doubled in volume.

Meanwhile, bring the milk and salt to a near boil, then allow the mixture to cool to lukewarm. Add the Butter Buds to the milk, then add this to the potato mixture. Beat ¾ cup of the egg substitute in a large bowl with the remaining sugar and mix in the potato mixture until well incorporated. Gradually add the flour until the mixture begins to come together into a dough. (You may not need all of the flour.) Place the dough in a large bowl that has been sprayed with nonstick cooking spray, cover with a clean towel, and set aside in a warm place to rise. When the dough has doubled in volume, divide it in half and place in two loaf pans and let rise again until doubled in size.

Preheat the oven to 350°.

Bake for 30 minutes and brush the remaining ¼ cup of egg substitute over the tops of the bread, then bake for an additional 10 minutes until golden brown and the bread makes a hollow sound when tapped.

Chapter 4

Lunches

Kids are notorious for not eating the lunch you've packed them—or for making less than nutritious selections at their school cafeteria. But if you pack one of these delicious lunches, you won't have to worry about your kids trading their food or throwing it away.

QUICK 'N' EASY LUNCHES

No time to cook? Here are lunches that even your child can prepare on his or her own.

Quick lunch 1:

▲ Peanut butter sandwich: 2 slices of whole-wheat bread, 1 tablespoon natural peanut butter, 2 teaspoons all-fruit jelly

▲ Baby carrots

▲ 8 ounces nonfat milk

Quick lunch 2:

▲ 1 whole-wheat bagel with 1 slice of nonfat cheese and 1 slice turkey breast

▲ Fruit (1 orange, 1 apple, or 1 small banana)

▲ 8 ounces nonfat milk

Quick lunch 3:

▲ 8 ounces nonfat yogurt with $\frac{1}{2}$ cup fruit and 8 almonds

▲ 3 graham cracker squares

▲ Celery stalks

Quick lunch 4:

▲ Energy bar (with at least 10 grams of protein)

▲ 1 piece of fruit

▲ 8 ounces nonfat milk

CRUNCHY PB IN A WRAP

VEGETARIAN

(Makes 4 servings)

Let's face it—traditional PB&J can be boring. Try shaking things up a bit by serving this classic combination in a tortilla wrap. It's easier to eat and travels well, and your kids will find it irresistible.

⅓ cup natural peanut butter

4 (10-inch) low-fat whole-wheat tortillas

1 cup chopped apple

¼ cup low-fat granola

Spread peanut butter over each tortilla and sprinkle with chopped apple and granola. Roll tortillas tightly and cut into halves. Serve immediately.

Calories 351
Protein 12 g
Carbohydrate 51 g
Fat 12 g

Food group servings:
Grain 1.25
Fruit 0.25
Protein 1.7
Fat 2.4

TORTILLAS, TORTILLAS, TORTILLAS

You'll find that our recipes suggest nonfat whole-wheat tortillas. What if you can't find nonfat or whole-wheat?

Depending on where you live, you may find only plain flour or corn tortillas—or you may find many varieties. You can choose different types; just pay attention to calorie content.

You may also enjoy lavash, a soft, thin flatbread made with wheat, flour, water, yeast, and salt.

TUNA SALAD

(Makes 8 servings)

Calories 92
Protein 13 g
Carbohydrate 8 g
Fat 1 g

Food group servings:
Protein 1.8
Fat 0.2

Tuna salad may not be the most glamorous lunch under the sun, but it has the distinction of being a low-calorie dream. There's no doubt it's delicious, but the key is to make it fun. When you're serving it at home, try stuffing this salad into a hollowed-out tomato or apple for a different twist on an old favorite. For a packed lunch, put it in a pita or a tortilla.

2	(6-ounce) cans tuna, packed in water	6	hard-boiled egg whites, chopped
½	cup nonfat mayonnaise	¼	teaspoon celery salt
½	cup sweet pickle relish	½	cup chopped celery

Combine all ingredients in a small bowl and chill.

SMASHED TURKEY SANDWICHES

(Makes 1 serving)

Calories 171
Protein 10 g
Carbohydrate 18 g
Fat 7 g

Food group servings:
Grain 1
Protein 1
Fat 1.4

These roll-ups are as fun to make as they are to eat. Your kids will enjoy squishing the bread with the rolling pin and helping you make these for lunch or an afternoon snack.

1	slice whole-grain bread	1	romaine lettuce leaf, washed and dried
1	tablespoon low-fat spreadable cream cheese	1	thin slice of tomato
1	slice smoked turkey breast	2	slices of avocado

Place the bread slice on a cutting board and cut off all four crusts. Using a rolling pin, gently flatten out the bread to form a long rectangle. Spread cream cheese over the flattened bread and top with a turkey slice and lettuce, then lay the tomato slice and avocado at one end of the bread. Starting at the tomato end, carefully roll the sandwich up and pat it gently to secure it. Serve whole or slice into pinwheels.

WHY WE LOVE AVOCADO

There's nothing like a ripe avocado to dress up a sandwich, wrap, or salad. This delicious fruit is rich in nutrients—packed with potassium, magnesium, folate, dietary fiber, riboflavin, and vitamins C, E, and B6. At least one study has suggested that avocado helps you absorb other nutrients in your meal.

Avocado has a "good" kind of fat, which helps you use important nutrients such as lutein and lycopene. Some studies suggest that the fat in avocados can reduce bad (low-density lipoprotein, or LDL) cholesterol and help raise good (high-density lipoprotein, or HDL) cholesterol.

A serving of one-fifth of an avocado has about 55 calories, 5 grams of fat, no cholesterol, and 3 grams of carbohydrate.

And it's delicious!

INSIDE-OUT TURKEY SANDWICHES

(Makes 4 servings)

Talk about a new twist on an old favorite! What better way to lift lunch out of the doldrums than to turn your child's favorite sandwich inside out?

12	slices turkey lunch meat	4	soft breadsticks (6 to 8 inches long)
½	cup low-fat cream cheese		Leaf lettuce

Calories 254
Protein 25 g
Carbohydrate 20 g
Fat 7 g

Food group servings:
Grain 1
Protein 3
Fat 1.4

Lay 3 turkey slices on a work surface, slightly overlapping each other so they measure the same length as the breadsticks. Spread the meat with 2 tablespoons of the cream cheese. Place one breadstick on the edge of the turkey and roll tightly. Roll 1 or 2 lettuce leaves around the outside of the sandwiches. Repeat with remaining ingredients to make 4 sandwiches. Wrap tightly in plastic wrap or serve immediately.

Calories 200
Protein 16 g
Carbohydrate 25 g
Fat 4 g

Food group servings:
Grain 1
Vegetable 0.25
Fruit 0.16
Protein 2
Fat 0.8

SPIRAL PINWHEEL SANDWICH

(Makes 1 serving)

Cold wrap sandwiches are perfect for lunch boxes. The tortilla stays nice and firm (nobody likes soggy bread), the sandwiches are easy to eat, and you can transform almost any combination of meat and/or vegetables into a wrap sandwich.

1   ounce very thinly sliced turkey lunch meat

1   slice low-fat American cheese, quartered

1   (10-inch) low-fat whole-wheat tortilla

2   teaspoons honey mustard

¼   cup shredded carrot

2   teaspoons dried cherries or raisins

Layer the turkey and the cheese on the tortilla. Spread the honey mustard on the turkey and top with the shredded carrot and cherries or raisins. Roll the tortilla tightly and cut in half. Wrap tightly in plastic wrap for later or serve immediately.

INVOLVE YOUR KIDS IN COOKING

Sure, your first inclination when trying to prepare a meal may be to shoo the kids out of the kitchen. But kids love to try cooking—and they're more likely to eat the foods they've helped prepare. With some help from you, your kids will be learning how to cook at the same time they're forming lifelong healthy eating habits.

Kids, depending on their ages, can help with just about any recipe. But here are recipes your child may find particularly appealing.

Brownie Fruit Pizza   page 178
California Roll-Up   page 49
Chocolate Chip Cookies   page 173

continued on next page

CUT-OUT TUNA SANDWICH SHAPES

(Makes 2 servings)

Cutting sandwiches into fun shapes is a great way to ignite your child's interest in eating a healthy lunch, and it goes a long way toward making mealtime fun. Let your kids pick their favorite shapes and cut out the bread—this way they get it exactly the way they like it.

1 (3-ounce) can chunk white tuna, packed in water	2 tablespoons plain low-fat yogurt
½ cup packaged shredded cabbage with carrot mix	2 tablespoons reduced-fat ranch salad dressing
	8 slices whole-grain bread

In a small bowl combine tuna, cabbage mix, yogurt, and ranch salad dressing. Using your child's favorite cookie cutter shapes, carefully cut out the bread shapes. Spread the tuna mixture on half of the bread cutouts and top with the remaining halves. Wrap tightly in plastic wrap or serve immediately.

Calories 223
Protein 17 g
Carbohydrate 30 g
Fat 5 g

Food group servings:
Grain 2
Vegetable 0.5
Protein 3
Fat 1.4

BROWN-BAGGING IT

Actually the brown bag is out—you'll probably want a lunch pack that's waterproof and that will hold several small containers. And let your child choose his or her own lunch bag. You may want to steer your child to one with a compartment for a freezer pack so you can send foods that need to be kept cool.

Your next goal is to pack a healthy lunch that not only doesn't take forever to prepare—but that your child will actually eat. As frustrating as it may be, food that your child deems boring or non-tasty will go straight in the trash.

Have a discussion with your children, and find out what they like and what they don't like about their lunches, and what they like about their friends' lunches. Ask if they ever skip lunch, and why. Younger kids may hurry through lunch to spend more time on the playground; the lunch line may be too long; kids may make fun of those bringing lunches from home.

Bear in mind that you're competing with the flashily wrapped snack packs and junk-food-laden lunch boxes of your child's peers. You're going to have to use some imagination to produce lunches that will appeal to your child, but this will become easier day by day. You'll find yourself automatically packing leftovers from dinner or breakfast into small containers to tuck into your child's lunch box.

Some ways to enliven your child's lunch:

FIND SANDWICH SUBSTITUTES. Instead of that standby sandwich, pack a whole-wheat bagel with low-fat cream cheese or nut butter; peanut butter and banana on whole-wheat bread; melted cheese with veggies on a whole-wheat tortilla; a roll-up or wrap (see pages 39–51); Boston Baked Beans (see page 103) in a thermos; or any soup, stew, or chili in a thermos.

SERVE SMALL PIECES. Especially for younger children, small foods are easier to eat. Cut sandwiches or tortillas into small, easy-to-handle pieces and cut veggies and fruit into small pieces. Put them in small containers that are easy for small fingers to open.

THINK CHIPS AND DIP. Kids love crunch—and it's easy to add it to a lunch. Pack sliced veggies or baked chips along with salsa, hummus, or a low-fat dressing.

USE SMALL CONTAINERS. If items get squished in your child's backpack or locker, invest in small plastic containers in which lunch items can be stored and protected.

CONSIDER TEMPERATURE. Many kids don't want to eat warm lunches. One way to keep lunches cool is to place a yogurt in the freezer the night before. Take the yogurt out in the morning and place in your child's lunch. It will keep the rest of the lunch cool, and by lunch time will be more like a frozen yogurt.

ANYTHING GOES. A lunch doesn't have to look like a lunch. You can pack leftover whole-grain waffles spread with peanut butter and sliced bananas, pizza, green beans with almonds, Cheerios, edamame, or leftover Tuna Noodle Casserole—whatever your child likes. Here are some other possibilities:

Red bell pepper strips	Fresh fruit: apples, peaches,
Celery with peanut butter	plums, bananas
Baby carrots with dressing	Canned fruit, packed in juice
Yogurt	Salads with low-fat dressing
Smoothies (see pages 69–74) in a thermos	Guacamole dip with baked chips
Nuts	Popcorn
Fruit, vegetable, or cheese kabobs	Trail mix
Cheese cubes, string cheese,	Muffins (see page 55)
or cottage cheese	Pretzels
Fruit salad	Rice cakes

PACK A DESSERT. If you don't, your child will buy one or get it from a friend—but if you pack a dessert, you can choose a healthy one. Pack homemade treats from the dessert chapter, low-fat granola bars, nonfat yogurt or pudding, or a small amount of chocolate chips mixed with nuts and raisins.

Calories 165
Protein 8 g
Carbohydrate 24 g
Fat 3.8 g

Food group servings:
Grain 1
Vegetable 1.4
Protein 1.4
Fat 1.8

PIZZA ROLLS
(Makes 6 servings)

You'll get no arguments when you pack these fantastic pizza rolls in your child's lunch box. Experiment by stuffing them with favorite topping combinations, such as Canadian bacon and pineapple. (You'll find pizza sauce in jars, usually next to marinara sauces.)

	Nonstick cooking spray		$\frac{1}{3}$	cup pizza sauce
	Cornmeal		3	(1-ounce) pieces low-fat string
1	(10-ounce) tube refrigerated			cheese, cut into halves
	pizza dough			crosswise
18	slices reduced-fat turkey			
	pepperoni			

Preheat the oven to 400°.

Spray a baking sheet with nonstick cooking spray and lightly sprinkle with cornmeal. Set aside.

On a lightly floured board press the pizza dough into a 13½ x 9-inch rectangle and cut the dough into six 4½-inch squares. Place 3 slices of turkey pepperoni in the center of each square and top with pizza sauce and string cheese. Bring the two opposite ends of the dough together and pinch to seal. Place seam side down on the prepared pan and bake for 15 to 18 minutes or until golden brown. If not serving immediately, cool completely and wrap in plastic wrap.

CURRIED CHICKEN BALLS

(Makes 2 servings, 4 chicken balls per serving)

Sometimes the best way to beat the lunchtime blues and ensure what you pack won't get traded is to experiment with the exotic. Try these curried chicken balls as a way to introduce a bit of globetrotting to your child's lunch hour. (If you can't find the mango chutney in your grocery store, you can substitute apricot preserves.)

½   **cup cooked chicken breast**

½   **teaspoon curry powder**

2   **teaspoons prepared mango chutney**

1   **teaspoon finely chopped flat-leaf parsley**

    Salt and pepper, to taste

Place the chicken, curry powder, mango chutney, parsley, salt, and pepper in the bowl of a food processor and pulse until finely chopped, about 30 seconds. Roll the chicken mixture into small balls (about an inch in diameter). Chill for several hours. Will keep for 3 to 4 days.

Calories 132
Protein 16g
Carbohydrate 4g
Fat 4g

Food group servings:

Protein 2.4
Fat 0.8

HAM AND CHEESE TURNOVERS

(Makes 9 servings)

Calories 158
Protein 10g
Carbohydrate 16g
Fat 6g

Food group servings:
Grain 1
Vegetable 0.1
Milk/Yogurt 0.13
Protein 1.4
Fat 1.2

Turnovers are a lot more fun than a traditional sandwich and they can be stuffed with an endless combination of fillings. You're limited only by your imagination!

Nonstick cooking spray
1¼ cups chopped cooked ham
1 cup small broccoli florets
¾ cup shredded Cheddar cheese

1 (10-ounce) tube refrigerated pizza dough
2 tablespoons nonfat milk

Preheat the oven to 400°.

Line a baking sheet with aluminum foil and spray lightly with nonstick cooking spray. Set aside. Combine the ham, broccoli, and cheese, and stir gently.

On a lightly floured surface roll the pizza dough into a 12-inch square. Using a sharp knife, cut the dough into 4-inch squares. Spoon about ⅓ cup of the filling onto one side of each square. Moisten the edges of the dough with a bit of water and fold one side over the other to form a turnover. Press the edges with the tines of a fork to seal. Prick a few holes in the top of each turnover to allow steam to escape. Brush the tops with milk and bake for 13 to 15 minutes or until golden. Serve warm.

CALIFORNIA ROLL-UP

(Makes 1 serving)

Calories 303
Protein 38 g
Carbohydrate 24 g
Fat 8 g

Food group servings:
Grain 1
Protein 5
Fat 1.6

The flavor combination in this roll-up is quintessential California. Feel free to experiment with a variety of flavored tortillas to keep things interesting. This portable package of good things is perfect for school lunch.

1   (10-inch) low-fat whole-wheat tortilla

4   slices deli shaved turkey breast

1   slice low-fat mozzarella cheese

4   thin slices cucumber

4   slices avocado

Alfalfa sprouts

Layer the tortilla with the turkey breast, cheese, cucumber, avocado, and a handful of sprouts. Roll it up and cut into halves. Wrap tightly in plastic wrap and refrigerate.

Calories 188
Protein 15 g
Carbohydrate 18 g
Fat 7 g

Food group servings:
Grain 1
Vegetable 0.2
Protein 2
Fat 1.4

CHICKEN PITA POCKETS

(Makes 4 servings)

You'll want some cooked chicken on hand to make these delicious pita pockets—either make a few extra chicken breasts when you prepare dinner, or buy a cooked chicken breast or two from your grocery store deli. Even a rotisserie chicken will do. (In a pinch you could use white meat canned chicken, packed in water.)

¼	cup plain low-fat yogurt	¼	cup shredded carrots
¼	cup reduced-fat ranch dressing	¼	cup chopped walnuts
1½	cups chopped cooked chicken breast	2	whole-wheat pita bread rounds, halved
½	cup chopped broccoli		Leafy lettuce

In a medium bowl combine the yogurt and ranch dressing. Stir in the chicken, broccoli, carrots, and walnuts and toss to coat. Line pita pockets with leafy lettuce; spoon mixture into pita pockets and serve.

CHICKEN TOMATO WRAP SANDWICH

(Makes 4 servings)

Calories 365
Protein 28 g
Carbohydrate 32 g
Fat 17 g

Food group servings:
Grain 1
Vegetable 0.25
Protein 4
Fat 3.4

By now you're starting to see that wraps are really more of a method than an exact recipe. As long as the ingredients you choose are fresh and low in fat, a wrap can be a healthy lunch. And because they can be filled with such a wide variety of fillings, you're sure to find the perfect combination to satisfy even a picky eater. This recipe is ideal for using up leftover chicken.

2	cups cubed cooked chicken breast	2	tomatoes, chopped
¼	cup honey Dijon salad dressing	4	(10-inch) low-fat whole-wheat or spinach tortillas
¼	cup nonfat mayonnaise	4	slices Muenster cheese
1	green bell pepper, chopped	4	lettuce leaves

In medium bowl combine the chicken, salad dressing, mayonnaise, bell pepper, and tomatoes, and toss to coat. Place the tortillas on a work surface and line with cheese and lettuce leaves. Divide the chicken mixture among tortillas and roll up tightly. Serve immediately or wrap tightly in plastic wrap and refrigerate.

WHAT ABOUT SCHOOL LUNCHES?

What if your child wants to buy lunch at school?

Your first thought may be, "Great! A healthy hot meal! (And I won't have to take time to pack a lunch.)"

You may want to think again. Many schools offer popular, fatty fare such as pizza, burgers, and fries, and most kids choose these foods over the salads or fruits that may also be available.

Visit the school and observe the possible choices, and discuss them at home with your child. Encourage your child to choose vegetables, salads, and fruit; whole-wheat bread instead of white; milk or water instead of juice or soda; baked food instead of fried. You may also ask your child to carry a lunch to school on one or two days a week.

If you are concerned about the meals being offered at your child's school, you may want to get involved to help work toward healthier lunches. If your child's school has soda and snack machines, you may want to lobby to have them removed or replaced with machines that sell milk or healthy snacks such as pretzels and apples.

CHAPTER 5

Snacks and Drinks

Kids get hungry—a lot. One of the KidShape themes is healthy regular snacking—basically eating five times a day! Besides breakfast, lunch, and dinner, your kids need at least two daily snacks to keep them going. This will keep their energy levels high and will mean they aren't "starving" when they reach mealtime.

Here are some healthy alternatives to the chips or cookies they may have been digging into, including some delicious frozen drink concoctions.

QUICK 'N' EASY SNACKS

▲ $\frac{1}{4}$ cup walnuts and $\frac{1}{2}$ cup blueberries

▲ 1 slice cheese and $\frac{1}{2}$ mango

▲ 1 tablespoon natural peanut butter and $\frac{1}{2}$ banana

▲ $\frac{1}{4}$ cup sunflower seeds

▲ $\frac{1}{4}$ cup cashews or almonds

▲ 2 tablespoons hummus on $\frac{1}{2}$ whole-wheat bagel

▲ 2 tablespoons hummus on whole-wheat pita with shredded carrots

▲ 2 tablespoons natural peanut butter on celery stalks

▲ 1 mini box raisins with $\frac{1}{4}$ cup soy nuts

▲ Low-fat granola bar with 6 ounces nonfat milk

▲ $\frac{1}{3}$ cup hummus with sliced carrots, bell pepper, and broccoli

▲ 1 slice Swiss cheese and 2 tablespoons raisins

▲ $\frac{1}{2}$ cup nonfat cottage cheese with $\frac{1}{2}$ cup unsweetened applesauce or $\frac{1}{2}$ cup pineapple

▲ 3 cups low-fat popcorn

▲ 1 string cheese and 1 small apple

▲ $\frac{1}{2}$ cup nonfat vanilla yogurt with $\frac{1}{3}$ cup blueberries

▲ 1 cup frozen grapes

▲ 1 cup nonfat cottage cheese with 1 tablespoon jam

▲ 1 peach

▲ 3 graham cracker squares with 1 tablespoon natural peanut butter

APPLE OAT BRAN MUFFINS

(Makes 12 servings)

Calories 124
Protein 3 g
Carbohydrate 16 g
Fat 3 g

Food group servings:
Grain 1
Protein 0.2
Fat 0.6

This is the perfect quick snack to hand a child heading out the door—tasty, easy to eat on the run, and nutritious.

1¼ cups whole-wheat flour

1 cup oat bran

⅓ cup packed brown sugar

2½ teaspoons baking powder

¼ teaspoon baking soda

¼ teaspoon salt

¼ teaspoon ground nutmeg

¼ teaspoon ground cinnamon

1 cup buttermilk

2 egg whites

2 tablespoons canola oil

¾ cup peeled and shredded apple
    Nonfat cooking spray

Preheat the oven to 425°.

In a medium bowl, stir together the flour, oat bran, brown sugar, baking powder, baking soda, salt, nutmeg, and cinnamon. In a small bowl combine the buttermilk, egg whites, and canola oil. Add the buttermilk mixture to the dry ingredients, stirring just until moistened. Stir in the shredded apple. (You can make this batter ahead of time and store it, tightly covered, in the refrigerator, for up to 5 days.) Coat a 12-cup muffin tin with nonfat cooking spray. Spoon about ¼ cup batter into each muffin cup. Bake for 18 to 20 minutes, or until a toothpick inserted in the middle comes out clean. Cool slightly, and remove the muffins from the tin.

VEGETARIAN

BAKED VEGETABLE QUESADILLAS

(Makes 10 servings)

This is a great low-fat alternative to a grilled cheese sandwich—and kids love quesadillas. The really good news is that you can make these ahead of time and keep them covered in the refrigerator and heat in the oven for a quick snack.

2   teaspoons olive oil

1   red bell pepper, thinly sliced

1   green bell pepper, thinly sliced

1   red onion, thinly sliced

½   teaspoon ground cumin

½   teaspoon chili powder

2   tablespoons chopped cilantro

⅓   cup low-fat shredded Cheddar cheese

5   (10-inch) low-fat whole-wheat tortillas

Salsa (optional)

Preheat the oven to 425°.

In a large nonstick skillet heat 1 teaspoon of the olive oil and sauté the peppers and the onion until crisp-tender. Add the cumin and chili powder, cooking and stirring for 1 minute more. Stir in the cilantro. Set aside.

Spread the vegetables over half of each tortilla. Sprinkle the cheese over the vegetables and fold the tortilla in half.

Place the tortillas on a baking sheet and brush them with the remaining 1 teaspoon of olive oil. Bake for 5 minutes until crisp and golden. Cut the quesadillas into 4 wedges. Serve warm topped with salsa.

MINI PIZZAS
(Makes 6 servings)

This delicious quick-and-easy snack is sure to be a big hit with your kids—and many kids can prepare it on their own (they can pop it in a toaster oven or microwave for 30 to 60 seconds instead of using the oven). For extra nutrition, choose whole-wheat English muffins.

6   English muffins, split in half

14   ounces low-fat pizza sauce

1   cup shredded low-fat mozzarella cheese

Preheat the oven to 400°.

Line a baking pan or baking sheet with aluminum foil. Arrange the muffin halves in the baking pan and spread 2 to 3 tablespoons of pizza sauce on each. Sprinkle with the mozzarella cheese. (Spread with vegetables such as mushrooms, onions, or bell peppers if desired.) Bake for 10 minutes or until cheese is bubbly. Serve hot.

Calories 245
Protein 14 g
Carbohydrate 31 g
Fat 7 g

Food group servings:
Grain 2
Protein 2
Fat 1

Calories 161
Protein 1 g
Carbohydrate 40 g
Fat 1 g

Food group servings:
Vegetable 0.2
Fruit 2
Fat 0.2

WALDORF SALAD

(Makes 6 servings)

This is a popular salad with kids because it's more like a dessert than a side dish. They love the crunch of the apples and walnuts paired with the sweetness of the honey and marshmallows. Come to think of it, it's popular with adults too. (You'll find rice vinegar in the Asian section of your grocery store, next to soy sauce.)

2	teaspoons unseasoned rice vinegar		1	cup halved seedless green grapes
¼	cup nonfat sour cream		2	cups mini marshmallows
¼	cup nonfat mayonnaise		1	cup chopped celery
1	teaspoon honey		½	cup raisins
3	cups cored and chopped apples			

In a small bowl combine rice vinegar, sour cream, mayonnaise, and honey. Toss the dressing with apples, grapes, marshmallows, celery, and raisins. Serve well chilled.

YOGURTY FRUIT SALAD

(Makes 12 servings)

Calories 145
Fat 1.7 g
Carbohydrates 32 g
Protein 4 g

Food group servings:
Milk/Yogurt 0.2
Fruit 2
Protein 0.2
Fat 1

You can entice even the pickiest child with this tasty treat that combines yogurt, banana, melon, pineapple, and strawberries (and, okay, lettuce, too, but the kids will hardly notice).

3 cups shredded leafy lettuce (not iceberg)

1 pint strawberries, halved

1 large banana, sliced

1 honeydew melon, cubed

1 (20-ounce) can pineapple chunks, drained

1 (8-ounce) carton nonfat vanilla yogurt

½ cup shredded Gruyere cheese

Put half the shredded lettuce in a large bowl. Layer the strawberries, banana, melon, and pineapple on top of the lettuce. Top with the remaining lettuce and spread the yogurt on top. Sprinkle with the cheese. Best if covered and chilled for 2 to 3 hours.

SPICY THAI NOODLES

(Makes 4 servings)

When I was visiting New York I fell in love with the cold peanut noodles from a great take-out place down the street from where I was staying. This made-over recipe is based on those noodles.

1¼ cups water	⅛ to ¼ teaspoon hot pepper flakes
2½ teaspoons brown sugar	¼ cup natural peanut butter
1 teaspoon garlic powder	¼ cup sliced green onions
2 teaspoons low-sodium soy sauce	1 tablespoon chopped cilantro
¾ teaspoon seasoned salt	8 ounces cooked linguine
½ teaspoon cornstarch	1½ cups shredded red cabbage

In a microwave-safe bowl, combine the water, brown sugar, garlic powder, soy sauce, seasoned salt, cornstarch, and hot pepper flakes. Microwave on high for 1 to 2 minutes, until bubbling. Stir in the peanut butter, green onions, and cilantro. Add the linguine and cabbage, and toss to coat in the sauce. Serve warm, at room temperature, or chilled.

BAKED ONION RINGS
(Makes 6 servings)

Calories 83
Protein 4 g
Carbohydrate 15 g
Fat 1 g

Food group servings:
Grain 0.7
Vegetable 0.6
Fat 0.2

These onion rings are crispy and crunchy and just as good as—if not better than—anything you'll find at a fast-food restaurant.

Nonstick cooking spray	¾ cup fine dry bread crumbs
2 medium yellow onions, cut into ¼-inch slices and separated into rings	3 tablespoons liquid Butter Buds
	¼ teaspoon salt
	2 egg whites, slightly beaten

Preheat the oven to 450°.

Spray a baking sheet with nonstick cooking spray and set aside. Cut the onions into ¼-inch slices and separate into rings. In a shallow dish combine the bread crumbs, Butter Buds, and salt. Dip the onion rings into the egg whites and then in the bread crumb mixture. Place them on the prepared baking sheet and bake for 12 to 15 minutes until the onions are tender and the coating is golden brown.

BAKED TORTILLA CHIPS

(Makes 14 servings, about 14 chips each)

The good news about making your own tortilla chips is that you control the salt and you can flavor them any way you like. Try cayenne pepper, Cajun spice, or even garlic powder. The possibilities are limitless—but the calories aren't!

10 **(10-inch) corn tortillas
(1 package)
Nonstick cooking spray**

**Ground cumin, to taste
Salt, to taste**

Preheat the oven to 375°.

Cut each tortilla into 20 triangles. Spread in a single layer on baking sheets, lightly coat with nonstick spray, and sprinkle with cumin and salt. Bake for about 10 minutes, turning once halfway through until golden and crispy. Bake in batches as necessary. Serve warm, or let cool and store in an airtight container.

BAKED POTATO SKINS

(Makes 4 servings)

These are a favorite at family restaurants, and for good reason—the combination of flavors is delectable. The standard version is, of course, loaded with fat, while this tasty version offers just over 200 calories per serving.

4	medium russet potatoes	2	tablespoons chopped fresh parsley
½	cup low-fat grated Cheddar cheese	4	green onions, thinly sliced
4	slices of crisp cooked turkey bacon, crumbled	¼	cup nonfat sour cream

Preheat the oven to 500°.

Pierce the potatoes in several places with a fork and microwave on high for 5 to 10 minutes until soft. Split the potatoes in half lengthwise, nest them in a clean kitchen towel, and carefully scoop out the pulp, leaving ¼ inch of potato on the skin—otherwise the skin won't hold its shape and will collapse. (Don't toss that scooped-out potato: it makes great mashed potatoes, or you can use it in the Hawaiian Sweet Bread recipe on page 36.)

Place the potato shells on a baking sheet and sprinkle with cheese, bacon, parsley, and green onion. Bake for 10 to 15 minutes until the potato skins are crispy and the cheese is bubbly. Serve immediately with a dollop of nonfat sour cream.

Calories 206
Protein 10 g
Carbohydrate 33 g
Fat 4 g

Food group servings:
Grain 2
Protein 1
Fat 0.8

Calories 78
Protein 1 g
Carbohydrate 19 g
Fat 0 g

Food group servings:
Fruit 1

OVEN-ROASTED FRUIT

(Makes 8 servings)

As with vegetables roasted at a high temperature, fruit becomes somehow fruitier as the flavors concentrate and the outside caramelizes. This is wonderful on its own or with a scoop of nonfat vanilla yogurt.

6   peaches, pitted and cut into eighths
6   plums, pitted and quartered
1   cup fresh raspberries
1   cup fresh blueberries
¼   cup sugar
2   tablespoons orange juice

Preheat the oven to 450°.

Arrange the fruit in a single layer, cut side up, in a large baking dish. Sprinkle with the sugar. Bake for 20 to 25 minutes until the fruit is tender.

Heat the broiler and place the fruit about 5 inches below the element and broil for 5 minutes until the fruit begins to caramelize. Remove from the broiler and sprinkle with the orange juice. Serve warm or at room temperature with a scoop of nonfat vanilla yogurt.

MORE SNACK RECIPES

In addition to foods we've singled out in this chapter for snacks, you'll find recipes throughout the book that can make great snacks. Here are some:

Banana Bread, page 34
Brownie Fruit Pizza, page 178
Hawaiian Sweet Bread, page 36
Individual Apple Crumble, page 185
Oatmeal Raisin Cookies, page 175
Pizza Rolls, page 46
Pumpkin Bread, page 34
Zucchini Bread, page 33

FROZEN FRUIT POPS

(Makes 8 servings)

Kids will love helping prepare these frozen pops—and they certainly love their sweet taste.

1   teaspoon unflavored gelatin
⅓   cup peach nectar
2   (16-ounce) containers nonfat
      vanilla yogurt

1   cup frozen fruit chunks (mango,
      peaches, or strawberries)

In a small saucepan combine the unflavored gelatin and the peach nectar. Allow to stand for 5 minutes, and then stir over medium heat until gelatin is dissolved.

Pour the gelatin mixture into a blender, along with the yogurt and frozen fruit chunks. Cover and blend until smooth. Pour the mixture into eight 3-ounce paper cups and cover each one with aluminum foil. Insert a wooden Popsicle stick into each cup and freeze for 4 to 6 hours or until firm.

To serve, remove foil and tear paper cups away from the pops.

Calories 83
Protein 7 g
Carbohydrate 14 g
Fat 0 g

Food group servings:
Milk/Yogurt 1
Fruit 1

FRUIT AND YOGURT PARFAIT

(Makes 2 servings)

Cool, creamy yogurt, crunchy granola and fresh fruit. What a combination! This can make a great breakfast or a yummy dessert as well as a healthy snack.

1   cup sliced fresh strawberries
½   cup low-fat granola

1   cup plain or vanilla nonfat
      yogurt

Place berries in the bottom of a shallow glass or bowl. Top with yogurt and sprinkle with granola. Serve chilled.

Calories 184
Protein 10 g
Carbohydrate 34 g
Fat 2 g

Food group servings:
Grain 1
Milk/Yogurt 0.5
Fruit 0.5
Fat 0.4

CHILLED STRAWBERRY SOUP
(Makes 8 servings)

Calories 84
Protein 3 g
Carbohydrate 17 g
Fat 1 g

Food group servings:
Milk/Yogurt 0.3
Fruit 0.5
Fat 0.2

Kids will love the idea of sipping a chilled soup from oversized mugs on a hot summer day. If you do the peeling and slicing, you can let the kids do the rest of the work—they especially love foods they've helped prepare.

1   fresh peach, peeled and sliced
1   nectarine, peeled and sliced
2   cups sliced strawberries
2   (8-ounce) cartons low-fat
    strawberry yogurt

2   tablespoons fresh lemon juice
    Chopped fresh mint leaves, for
    garnish

In a blender, combine peach, nectarine, and strawberry slices with yogurt and lemon juice. Process until smooth. Cover and refrigerate. Spoon into soup bowls and garnish with mint.

FRESH FRUIT DIP
(Makes 4 servings)

Calories 173
Protein 7 g
Carbohydrate 14 g
Fat 10 g

Food group servings:
Fruit 1
Fat 2

This recipe is easy and satisfies a child's sweet tooth—and supplies healthy fresh fruit as well.

1   (8-ounce) package low-fat
    cream cheese, room temperature
1   (7-ounce) jar marshmallow
    cream

2   cups assorted fresh fruit:
    apples, pineapple, strawberries,
    and whatever you like

In a small bowl beat together the cream cheese and the marshmallow cream with an electric mixer until smooth and well combined. Serve with the fresh fruit for dipping!

ONION DIP

(Makes 4 servings, ½ cup per serving)

Everyone loves creamy onion dip. Serve this with cut-up vegetables and watch your kids make them disappear.

2 cups nonfat sour cream	1 envelope dry onion soup mix

In a small bowl combine the sour cream and the soup mix. Mix well and chill for at least an hour to allow the flavors to develop. Serve with fresh vegetables.

Calories 123
Protein 5 g
Carbohydrate 25 g
Fat 1 g

Food group servings:
Milk/Yogurt 0.6
Fat 0.2

HOT ARTICHOKE DIP

(Makes 8 servings)

Kids love this—believe it or not! Serve with fresh sliced carrots, celery, and bell pepper, or baked tortilla chips.

Nonstick cooking spray	1 teaspoon fresh lemon juice
2 (14-ounce) cans artichoke hearts	1 garlic clove, chopped
1 cup light mayonnaise	5 drops Tabasco sauce
½ cup grated Parmesan cheese	1 cup grated mozzarella cheese

Calories 184
Protein 10 g
Carbohydrate 14 g
Fat 11 g

Food group servings:
Vegetable 0.5
Protein 0.2
Fat 2.2

Preheat the oven to 350°.

Spray a casserole dish with nonstick cooking spray and set aside. Meanwhile, in a large bowl combine the artichoke hearts, mayonnaise, Parmesan cheese, lemon juice, garlic, Tabasco sauce, and mozzarella cheese and pour the mixture into the prepared casserole dish. Bake for 15 to 20 minutes until hot and bubbly.

Drinks

Sometimes a tasty beverage is just what a kid needs for an after-school snack—or you can combine a drink with a sandwich or wrap for a complete meal.

Calories 100
Protein 5 g
Carbohydrate 17 g
Fat 1 g

Food group servings:
Milk/Yogurt 0.5
Fat 0.2

 ## KICKED-UP HOT CHOCOLATE
(Makes 2 servings)

As a kid growing up in sunny California, I would use the slightest drop in temperature or the slightest breeze as an excuse to make hot chocolate. Now I don't need an excuse. This hot chocolate is great any time of the year.

1 cup hot water	¼ teaspoon ground cinnamon
2 teaspoons sugar	2 tablespoons reduced-calorie whipped topping
1 cup nonfat milk	
2 (0.55-ounce) envelopes nonfat hot cocoa mix	1 maraschino cherry, halved

In a large, microwave-safe glass measuring cup, combine water, sugar, milk, cocoa, and cinnamon. Stir well. Microwave on high for 90 seconds. Pour cocoa into 2 mugs and top each with 1 tablespoon whipped topping and a maraschino cherry half.

CLASSIC ORANGE JULIUS

(Makes 2 servings)

Calories 212
Protein 7 g
Carbohydrate 47 g
Fat 0 g

Food group servings:
Milk/Yogurt 0.5
Fruit 3

Everyone loves a classic—especially with none of the fat and all of the flavor. Whip up this cool and creamy treat for your kids as a satisfying dessert or a quick snack on the way to soccer practice.

½ (12-ounce) can orange juice
   concentrate

1 cup nonfat milk

½ teaspoon vanilla
   Handful of ice

In a blender combine orange juice concentrate, milk, vanilla, and ice. Blend on high speed until smooth and serve immediately.

A VERY BERRY SMOOTHIE

(Makes 3 servings)

Calories 141
Protein 5 g
Carbohydrate 31 g
Fat 0.6 g

Food group servings:
Milk/Yogurt 0.5
Fruit 1.6
Fat 0.13

This should be called the "everything but the kitchen sink" drink. It's definitely got something for everyone.

1½ cups nonfat milk

1   cup fresh or frozen berries
    (strawberries, blueberries,
    raspberries)

1   ripe banana, sliced

2   tablespoons orange juice
    concentrate

1   cup ice

Place all ingredients in blender and blend until smooth. Serve immediately.

VANILLA BERRY SMOOTHIE

(Makes 2 servings)

The addition of vanilla in this drink somehow brings out the "berriness" of the berries.

1½ cups nonfat milk
1 cup fresh berries (strawberries, blueberries, raspberries)
1 teaspoon vanilla

2 teaspoons cinnamon
2 teaspoons honey
1 cup ice

Place all ingredients in blender and blend until smooth. Serve immediately.

PINEAPPLE-GINGER SMOOTHIE

(Makes 2 servings)

The fresh ginger in this smoothie gives it an unexpected kick.

1½ cups nonfat milk
6 ounces grape juice
6 ounces canned crushed pineapple, drained

1 teaspoon grated ginger
1 cup ice

Place all ingredients in blender and blend until smooth. Serve immediately.

COCONUT-STRAWBERRY SMOOTHIE

(Makes 2 servings)

Your kids will love this cool and creamy concoction.

1½	cups nonfat milk	6	fresh or frozen strawberries
1	ripe banana, sliced	2	tablespoons canned coconut cream (sweetened)

Place all ingredients in blender and blend until smooth. Serve immediately.

Calories 157
Protein 7 g
Carbohydrate 25 g
Fat 4 g

Food group servings:
Milk/Yogurt 0.75
Fruit 1.1
Fat 0.8

PEANUT BUTTER DELIGHT

(Makes 2 servings)

Think peanut butter cup in a glass with a banana twist.

1½	cups nonfat milk	4	tablespoons powdered chocolate drink mix
2	tablespoons natural peanut butter	1	cup ice
1	ripe banana, sliced		

Place all ingredients in blender and blend until smooth. Serve immediately.

Calories 207
Protein 9 g
Carbohydrate 31 g
Fat 7 g

Food group servings:
Milk/Yogurt 0.75
Fruit 1
Fat 1.4

BANANA-PINEAPPLE LICUADO

(Makes 3 servings)

Calories 157
Protein 4 g
Carbohydrate 37 g
Fat 0.7 g

Food group servings:
Milk/Yogurt 0.3
Fruit 2.2
Fat 0.13

A smoothie by any other name . . . you'll love licuados, which are blender beverages originating in Mexico and Central and Latin America, made with cold milk and fresh fruit. This combination is just the cool and refreshing drink you'd want if you were stranded on a deserted tropical island.

1   cup nonfat milk

1   ripe banana, sliced

2   cups canned pineapple chunks, drained

1   cup ice

Place all ingredients in blender and blend until smooth. Serve immediately.

PURPLE MOO

(Makes 2 servings)

Calories 186
Protein 7 g
Carbohydrate 40 g
Fat 1 g

Food group servings:
Milk/Yogurt 0.75
Fruit 1
Fat 0.2

Kids love the vibrant purple color of this cool and creamy treat.

1½ cups nonfat milk

1   cup fresh or frozen blueberries

1   tablespoon all-fruit jam

2   tablespoons honey

1   cup ice

Place all ingredients in blender and blend until smooth. Serve immediately.

STRAWBERRY LICUADO

(Makes 2 servings)

This drink is the ultimate for strawberry lovers.

1	cup nonfat milk	2	teaspoons sugar
1½	cups fresh strawberries	½	cup ice

Place all ingredients in blender and blend until smooth. Serve immediately.

Calories 99
Protein 5 g
Carbohydrate 19 g
Fat 1 g

Food group servings:
Milk/Yogurt 0.5
Fruit 1
Fat 0.2

ADDING FIBER TO YOUR MEALS

Kids have a tendency not to get enough fiber, not enough fruits and vegetables, and sometimes not enough protein. But by adding certain ingredients you can add extra nutritional value to your kids' favorite foods.

One way to do this is by adding vegetables, chopped finely or even blended, into sauces; for example, you could add chopped carrots or zucchini to spaghetti sauce. Smoothies are a great way to blend additional fruit servings into your child's diet. And you can add soy protein powder to those same smoothies for extra protein. Adding ground flax seed to cereals, smoothies, and soups adds nutritious protein, antioxidants, fiber, and omega 3 fatty acids.

Be creative!

TROPICAL PINEAPPLE SMOOTHIE

(Makes 3 servings)

The more fruit, the merrier. Kids love this combination of fruit and sherbet.

1	cup pineapple juice	¼	cup nonfat plain yogurt
1	cup frozen strawberries	1	cup pineapple sherbet
½	cup frozen bananas	½	cup ice

Pour the pineapple juice in the blender. Add the strawberries, bananas, yogurt, sherbet, and ice. Blend until smooth.

Calories 190
Protein 3 g
Carbohydrate 42 g
Fat 2 g

Food group servings:
Fruit 2.8
Fat 0.4

BANANA-HONEY SMOOTHIE

(Makes 4 servings)

The avocado adds some calories but lots of nutrients, and you and your kids will love the blend of flavors. Enjoy!

1	cup orange juice	1	tablespoon honey
1	ripe avocado	1	cup nonfat frozen yogurt
1	ripe banana		(vanilla, orange, or peach)

Put the orange juice, avocado, banana, and honey in blender, and blend until smooth. Add the frozen yogurt and blend until thick and smooth.

Calories 208
Protein 5 g
Carbohydrate 42 g
Fat 3.5 g

Food group servings:
Milk/Yogurt 0.25
Fruit 0.6
Fat 7

CHAPTER 6

Main Dishes

What's for dinner?" It's a refrain you've probably heard far too often. Here are some wonderful choices, including healthy versions of classic kids' favorites. You'll find something to tease even the choosiest of palates.

QUICK 'N' EASY DINNERS

Soccer games and school plays and late meetings at work—sometimes there isn't time to read a recipe, let alone cook a meal. Resist the urge to call for take-out or stop at a fast-food restaurant—here are some meals you can toss together in minutes.

Quick dinner 1:

▲ Whole-wheat pasta

▲ Spaghetti sauce (keep some in your pantry; read labels to choose brands with no corn syrup) with ground beef (cook it before adding the sauce or keep some cooked in your freezer for these occasions—you can also toss in chopped veggies)

▲ Tossed salad with low-fat dressing

Quick dinner 2:

▲ Mix water-packed tuna with chopped-up celery, relish, and 2 tablespoons nonfat yogurt

▲ Baby carrots

▲ Whole-wheat rolls

▲ Fresh fruit with nonfat nondairy topping

Quick dinner 3:

▲ Baked potatoes, prepared in the microwave, with low-fat cheese and strips of ham on top

▲ Tossed salad with low-fat dressing

PINEAPPLE BEEF

(Makes 4 servings)

Calories 192
Protein 20 g
Carbohydrate 16 g
Fat 5 g

Food group servings:
Vegetable 0.5
Fruit 0.25
Protein 2.7
Fat 1

In about the time it takes to order Chinese take-out, you can pull together this quick and healthy dish for a midweek dinner. Kids like the sweetness that the pineapple adds, and with a side of steamed rice, this makes a satisfying and complete meal.

12	ounces beef top round steak	1	tablespoon cornstarch
1	(8-ounce) can pineapple slices in juice		Nonstick cooking spray
		1	cup fresh snow peas
2	tablespoons reduced-sodium soy sauce	4	green onions, cut into ½-inch pieces
½	teaspoon ground ginger	1	medium plum tomato, cut into wedges
¼	teaspoon red pepper flakes		

Partially freeze the beef for easier slicing and cut across the grain into thin strips. Drain the pineapple, reserving juice, and cut pineapple rings into quarters.

In a small bowl combine the pineapple juice, soy sauce, ground ginger, and red pepper flakes. Add the meat and toss to coat in the marinade. Allow the flavors to develop for 15 minutes at room temperature. Drain the meat, reserving the excess marinade for the sauce. Add the cornstarch to the marinade.

Lightly coat a large nonstick skillet with cooking spray and place over medium-high heat. Add the beef and cook for 2 to 3 minutes until desired doneness. Push the meat to the edges of the skillet and add the reserved marinade to the pan. Bring the sauce to a bubble, and cook, stirring until thickened. Add the pineapple, snow peas, green onions, and tomato. Cook for 2 minutes more. Serve immediately with steamed rice.

BEEF AND VEGGIE STIR-FRY

(Makes 4 servings)

Calories 131
Protein 14 g
Carbohydrate 7 g
Fat 2 g

Food group servings:
Vegetable 1
Protein 2
Fat 0.4

Loaded with flavor but not oil, this quick and colorful stir-fry is sure to become a family favorite. The secret is not to overcook the vegetables: stir-fry them until they are slightly tender but still crisp.

¾	pound beef round steak, boneless	⅛	teaspoon garlic powder
1	teaspoon olive oil	1	dash black pepper
½	cup sliced carrots	2	cups zucchini squash, cut in thin strips
½	cup sliced onion	1	tablespoon cornstarch
1	tablespoon soy sauce	¼	cup water

Trim fat from steak. Slice steak across the grain into strips about ⅛ inch wide and 3 inches long (partially frozen meat is easier to slice). Heat oil in a frying pan. Add beef strips and stir-fry over high heat about 3 to 5 minutes, turning pieces constantly, until beef is no longer red. Reduce heat. Add carrots, onion, and seasonings. Cover and cook 3 to 4 minutes until carrots are slightly tender. Add squash and cook 3 to 4 minutes until vegetables are crisp-tender. Mix cornstarch and water until smooth, and add it slowly to beef mixture, stirring constantly. Cook until thickened and vegetables are coated with a thin glaze.

For a variation, you can use 3 boneless, skinless chicken breast halves without bone or skin instead of beef. Slice into thin strips. Cook the chicken until thoroughly done or no longer pink in color.

BEEF STROGANOFF

(Makes 7 servings)

Why not take your kids on a trip to Russia in the middle of an otherwise dull school week? This meal is just the ticket. This is a very quick-cooking recipe— it can be on the table in less than 30 minutes, with only about 5 minutes of cooking time. The meat is cut up small and the idea is to sear it for a little color and flavor.

Calories 205
Protein 16 g
Carbohydrate 26 g
Fat 4 g

Food group servings:
Grain 1.1
Vegetable 0.6
Protein 2
Fat 0.8

	Nonstick cooking spray	2	garlic cloves, minced
1	pound beef eye of round, cut into ½-inch cubes	3	cups beef broth
	Salt and pepper, to taste	1	cup nonfat sour cream
2	medium onions, chopped	4	cups medium-size yolk-free egg noodles
8	ounces sliced mushrooms		

Spray a large skillet with nonstick cooking spray and place over medium-high heat until almost smoking. Season the meat with salt and pepper and cook for about a minute on each side (turning only once). Allow the meat to brown on the outside, but don't overcook, as it will finish cooking in the sauce. Remove the meat from the pan and set aside. Add the onions, mushrooms, and garlic to the pan and cook, stirring occasionally, for about 5 minutes until mushrooms release their liquid and onions are translucent.

Whisk in the beef broth, making sure to scrape up any browned bits from the bottom of the pan. Gently stir in the sour cream and fold in the meat and egg noodles. Increase the heat to high and bring the sauce to boil. Reduce heat and simmer, uncovered, for 5 to 7 minutes until the pasta is al dente and the meat is cooked through. Remove from the heat and let stand for 4 to 5 minutes before serving. The sauce will thicken upon standing.

TURKEY BURGERS

(Makes 8 servings)

In our busy lives it's nice to have a few "go to" recipes that are refreshingly uncomplicated, low in fat, and of course delicious. This is just that kind of recipe—just plan ahead a bit, so that you can refrigerate the patties for 30 minutes before cooking. You can find inexpensive grill pans at department stores, or you could sear the burgers in a nonstick pan sprayed with cooking spray. Or fire up your outdoor grill.

2   **pounds ground white meat turkey**

¾   **cup grated zucchini**

2   **(8-ounce) cans sliced mushrooms, drained and chopped**

1   **envelope dried onion soup mix**

½   **cup barbecue sauce**

In a large bowl combine the turkey, zucchini, mushrooms, and onion soup mix. Form the meat into 8 equal patties and refrigerate for 30 minutes before cooking. Preheat an indoor grill pan over medium-high heat and grill burgers for 5 to 7 minutes per side, until cooked through. Baste the burgers with barbecue sauce during last few minutes of cooking.

CHILI TURKEY BURGERS

(Makes 4 servings)

Calories 253
Protein 42 g
Carbohydrate 6 g
Fat 6 g

Food group servings:
Vegetable 0.5
Protein 6
Fat 1.2

Those of us who live in Southern California have the pleasure and sometimes the curse of eating at a famous local chain that serves (as far as I'm concerned) the best chili burgers on the planet. I say "curse" because if you had any idea how much fat and calories just one of those burgers holds you'd (hopefully) never eat one again. I'm convinced that one of the things that makes them taste so good is that they are served wrapped in waxed paper, and at the original walk-up restaurant you eat them standing up, elbow to elbow with your neighbor, chili dripping off your chin. In an effort to keep my favorite foods, while trying to maintain a healthier lifestyle, I present you a much healthier version of that glorious burger—with all of the flavors and only a fraction of the fat.

1 pound ground white turkey breast	2 tablespoons crushed barbecue-flavor baked potato chips
1 cup canned tomatoes with green chilies	1 tablespoon tomato paste
½ cup medium diced onions	½ tablespoon salt
2 garlic cloves, minced	4 ounces sliced low-fat Cheddar cheese
1 tablespoon chili powder	

Preheat stovetop or outdoor grill to medium-high.

In a medium bowl combine the turkey, tomatoes, onions, garlic, chili powder, crushed chips, tomato paste, and salt. Smoosh the turkey mixture together with clean hands until mixture is well combined. Form into 4 equal patties and place on the preheated grill. Cook for 5 minutes per side, or until cooked through and no longer pink in the middle. Remove the patties from the grill and top each with a slice of cheese. Loosely tent with foil and allow the patties to rest and the cheese to melt. Serve hot.

TURKEY MEAT LOAF

(Makes 10 servings)

Calories 147
Protein 17 g
Carbohydrate 13 g
Fat 3 g

Food group servings:
Grain 0.3
Protein 1.5
Fat 0.6

You can't get much more "down home" than meat loaf. It's a definite crowd pleaser and so easy to put together. The oven does all the work! Just be sure to use ground white meat turkey breast to keep this recipe lean.

	Nonstick cooking spray	1	teaspoon salt
1	pound ground white turkey meat	1	teaspoon black pepper
½	cup egg substitute	1	envelope dry onion soup mix
½	cup plain bread crumbs	1	(8-ounce) can tomato sauce
¾	cup ketchup		

Preheat the oven to 350°.

Spray a metal or glass loaf pan with nonstick cooking spray and set aside. In a large bowl combine the ground turkey, egg substitute, bread crumbs, ketchup, salt and pepper, and onion soup mix, being careful not to overwork the meat. Pat the meat mixture into the prepared pan and spread the tomato sauce over the top. Bake for one hour.

SHEPHERD'S PIE

(Makes 8 servings)

Always a favorite with kids—and it makes great leftovers.

Calories 382
Protein 32 g
Carbohydrate 28 g
Fat 16 g

Food group servings:
Grain 1.8
Meat 2
Fat 3

For the mashed potato topping:

- 2 pounds potatoes, such as russet, peeled and cubed
- 2 tablespoons nonfat sour cream
- ¼ cup egg substitute
- ¼ cup evaporated skim milk
  Salt and freshly ground black pepper, to taste

For the meat and veggie filling:

- 1 tablespoon extra-virgin olive oil
- 1¾ pounds ground turkey breast
- 1 carrot, peeled and chopped
- 1 onion, chopped
- 2 tablespoons all-purpose flour
- 1 cup beef stock or broth
- 2 teaspoons Worcestershire sauce
- ½ cup frozen peas
- 1 teaspoon paprika
- 2 tablespoons chopped fresh parsley leaves, for garnish

Place the potatoes in a large pot of cold water, bring to a boil, and cook until tender, about 12 minutes. Salt the water once it begins to boil.

Meanwhile, preheat a large skillet over medium-high heat. Add the oil and the turkey to the pan and season with salt and pepper. Brown and crumble meat for 3 or 4 minutes. Add the chopped carrot and onion to the meat. Cook veggies with meat 5 minutes, stirring frequently. Sprinkle the flour over the meat mixture and cook for 1 minute to get rid of the raw taste of the flour. Whisk in the broth and Worcestershire sauce and bring the mixture to a boil and allow it to thicken for 1 minute. Stir in the peas.

Drain the potatoes and pour them into a bowl. Combine sour cream, egg substitute, and evaporated skim milk and mash into the potatoes until almost smooth.

Preheat the broiler.

Fill a small rectangular casserole dish with the meat and vegetable mixture. Spoon potatoes evenly over the top. Run a fork over the top of the potatoes to make ridges. Sprinkle potatoes with paprika and broil 6 to 8 inches from the heat until potatoes are evenly browned. Top with chopped parsley and serve.

TURKEY TACO SALAD

(Makes 4 servings)

Calories 400
Protein 40 g
Carbohydrate 48 g
Fat 6 g

Food group servings:
Grain 0.5
Vegetable 1
Protein 5
Fat 1.2

Kids love taco salad! Because this is made with ground turkey, it's much leaner than the ground beef version. But your kids will never taste the difference.

Nonstick cooking spray

12 ounces ground turkey breast

1 (15-ounce) can pinto beans, rinsed and drained

1 cup whole corn kernels

1 cup salsa

¼ cup water

4 to 6 cups shredded lettuce

¼ cup grated low-fat Cheddar cheese

1 cup broken baked tortilla chips

Lightly spray a nonstick skillet with cooking spray and place over medium heat. Cook the ground turkey for about 5 minutes or until no longer pink. Drain off any excess fat. Stir in the beans, corn, salsa, and water. Bring to a boil. Reduce the heat and simmer, covered, for 2 to 3 minutes to thicken.

Line 4 plates with shredded lettuce. Top with hot turkey mixture and sprinkle with cheese and tortilla chips. Serve immediately.

EASY TURKEY CHIMICHANGAS

(Makes 8 servings)

Calories 315
Protein 26 g
Carbohydrate 28 g
Fat 10 g

Food group servings:
Grain 1
Vegetable 0.7
Protein 0.8
Fat 2

A chimichanga, in case you didn't know, is traditionally a deep-fried burrito and one of the tastiest forms of Mexican food. The problem, of course, is the huge amount of fat and calories it packs. Fear not. Now you can have your chimichanga and eat it too! (Note: Chipotles are smoked jalapeño peppers that come in a can and are available in the Mexican or international foods section of the grocery store. These are hot! Use one for moderate heat, two for really hot chimichangas.)

4   (12-inch) low-fat whole-wheat tortillas

1   pound thickly sliced smoked deli turkey, chopped

1   tablespoon chili powder

2   cups shredded slaw cabbage

1   to 2 chipotles in adobo sauce

1   cup tomato sauce

3   green onions, chopped
    Salt and pepper, to taste

1½ cups shredded low-fat Cheddar cheese

2   tablespoons olive oil, for brushing

1   cup nonfat sour cream

2   tablespoons chopped cilantro, for garnish

1   large tomato, seeded and finely chopped

Preheat the oven to 400°.

Wrap tortillas in foil and place in the oven to heat through. Meanwhile, place the turkey in a bowl and season with chili powder. Add the shredded cabbage, chipotle chilis, tomato sauce, and green onions. Toss the filling to combine and season with salt and pepper.

To make the chimichangas, place one-fourth of the cheese near one edge of the tortilla. Pile one-fourth of your filling alongside the cheese. Tuck the sides up and roll the tortilla tightly. Repeat to make 4 large stuffed tortilla wraps. Brush the wraps with olive oil and bake until deep golden in color, 15 to 17 minutes. Top with the sour cream, cilantro, and chopped tomato. Cut in half and serve.

SCRUMPTIOUS CHILI DOGS

(Makes 1 serving)

What kid can resist a good chili dog? For that matter, what adult? With a few simple modifications, your kids can still enjoy their messy favorite.

1   turkey hot dog

1   whole-wheat hot dog bun

¼   cup Vegetarian Chili (see page 140)

1   tablespoon grated low-fat Cheddar cheese

1   tablespoon chopped red onion

Score the hot dog diagonally in a few places and cook on high in the microwave for 1 minute. Heat the chili in a microwave-safe bowl for 1 minute. Place the hot dog in the bun and pour the chili over the top. Sprinkle with grated cheese and onion.

BARBECUED CHICKEN
(Makes 8 servings)

Calories 176
Protein 22 g
Carbohydrate 14 g
Fat 3 g

Food group servings:
Protein 3
Fat 0.6

It's so much more satisfying to make your own sauces than to buy them in a bottle. I know what you're thinking: "Who has that kind of time or energy at the end of the day?" Relax! In truth this recipe uses bottled sauce, but it's enhanced with a few bolder flavors to make it your own. You can put it together in the first 10 minutes the chicken spends in the oven.

	Nonstick cooking spray	¼	cup ketchup
8	boneless, skinless chicken breasts	¼	cup orange juice
¼	teaspoon salt	2	tablespoons lightly packed brown sugar
¼	teaspoon black pepper	2	tablespoons light molasses
2	teaspoons liquid Butter Buds	6	dashes hot pepper sauce (optional)
2	garlic cloves, minced		
¾	cup bottled barbecue sauce		

Preheat the oven to 375°.

Spray a baking sheet with nonstick cooking spray and arrange the chicken breasts on it; season with salt and pepper. Bake for 10 minutes.

Meanwhile, in a medium saucepan heat the Butter Buds over medium heat and cook the garlic for 30 seconds. Stir in the barbecue sauce, ketchup, orange juice, brown sugar, molasses, and hot pepper sauce. Simmer for 5 minutes.

Brush the chicken breasts with barbecue sauce on both sides and bake for 10 to 15 more minutes or until chicken is no longer pink in the middle (180°). Serve immediately with remaining sauce.

FAST FAJITAS

(Makes 4 servings)

This fast-food favorite gets a healthy makeover—but retains its taste.

4   (10-inch) low-fat spinach or whole-wheat tortillas
    Nonstick cooking spray
12 ounces boneless, skinless chicken breasts, cut into bite-size pieces
⅓   cup finely chopped onion
⅓   cup finely chopped red or green bell pepper
½   cup chopped tomato
2   tablespoons bottled low-calorie Italian salad dressing
½   cup grated low-fat Cheddar cheese
¼   cup bottled salsa
¼   cup nonfat sour cream

Preheat the oven to 350°.

Wrap tortillas in foil and place in the oven for about 10 minutes, until heated through. Meanwhile, spray a large nonstick skillet with nonstick cooking spray. Add the chicken, onion, pepper, and tomato and cook for 5 to 7 minutes until the chicken is cooked through. Remove from heat and stir in the Italian dressing.

To serve, fill warm tortillas with chicken mixture and roll up. Serve cheese, salsa, and sour cream on the side.

OVEN-BAKED CHICKEN
(Makes 4 servings)

Calories 309
Protein 29 g
Carbohydrate 29 g
Fat 7 g

Food group servings:
Grain 1
Protein 4
Fat 1.4

Crispy, crunchy chicken from the oven that tastes like it's from the deep fryer? No kidding! The secret here is Melba toast, which adds great crunch— and the Dijon mustard adds wonderful tang. Your kids will love this one.

½   **cup egg substitute**

1   **tablespoon Dijon mustard**

1   **teaspoon dried thyme**

¾   **teaspoon salt**

½   **teaspoon black pepper**

4   **boneless, skinless chicken breasts**

1   **(5¼-ounce) package plain Melba toast, crushed**

    Nonstick cooking spray

Preheat the oven to 400°.

Place a large wire cooling rack on a foil-lined baking sheet and set aside. Mix egg substitute, mustard, thyme, salt, and pepper in a shallow dish. Roll the chicken breasts in the egg mixture, then roll to coat in the crushed Melba crumbs, pressing into the chicken. Shake off the excess and place on the wire rack. Spray the chicken lightly with the nonstick cooking spray and bake for 25 to 30 minutes until the coating is golden brown and the juices of the chicken run clear.

CHICKEN WITH DIJON AND APRICOT SAUCE

(Makes 4 servings)

Calories 320
Protein 32 g
Carbohydrate 31 g
Fat 8 g

Food group servings:
Milk/Yogurt 0.25
Protein 3.4
Fat 1.4

Just when you thought you couldn't do anything else with chicken. This is a great easy recipe for a quick dinner your kids are sure to love.

4	boneless, skinless chicken breasts	2	garlic cloves, minced
	Salt and pepper, to taste	1	teaspoon curry powder
1	tablespoon olive oil	2	tablespoons Dijon-style mustard
½	cup chicken broth	½	cup apricot preserves
1	cup chopped onions	½	cup plain nonfat yogurt

Season the chicken with salt and pepper. In a medium skillet heat the olive oil over medium-high heat and lightly brown the chicken for 3 to 5 minutes per side. Remove from pan and set aside.

Add a few tablespoons of the chicken broth to the pan and sauté the onions and garlic until soft, about 5 minutes. Add the curry powder, mustard, apricot preserves, and remaining chicken broth. Bring the sauce to a bubble and return the chicken to the pan. Cover, reduce heat, and simmer 10 to 15 minutes until chicken is just cooked through. Stir the yogurt into the sauce and serve immediately.

CHICKEN STOCK EXPLAINED

Chicken stock is simply chicken bones, a few vegetables, and some onions, garlic, and spices simmered for several hours in a big pot of water. Some call it "stock," others call it "broth." Really and truly, the end result is the same no matter what you call it. There are many great brands of commercial stocks and broths on the market and they are all readily available. You could make your own homemade stock, but that's a lot of effort. Avoid using bouillon unless that's all you have available—it will do in a pinch, but it tastes very salty and tends to be full of preservatives, sodium, and unpronounceable ingredients that you probably don't really want to feed to your children.

CHICKEN BREASTS VERONIQUE

(Makes 4 servings)

Don't let the French name of this recipe intimidate you. This dish is deceptively easy to make and can be ready in less than half an hour. Your kids will be intrigued by the addition of grapes, and it's sure to become one of your family favorites. (If you prefer not to use the wine—the alcohol does cook out—you can substitute chicken broth, for a somewhat different but still delicious flavor.)

2	tablespoons olive oil	½	cup evaporated skim milk
4	boneless, skinless chicken breasts	2	teaspoons each cornstarch and water, stirred together
1½	tablespoons orange marmalade	1½	cups seedless green grapes, halved
½	teaspoon dried tarragon		
½	cup dry white wine (the alcohol cooks out)		

In a large skillet heat the olive oil until almost smoking. Add the chicken and sear for a few minutes until golden on each side. Remove from the pan and stir in the marmalade, tarragon, and wine, and bring to a boil, scraping up any brown bits from the bottom of the pan. Return the chicken to the pan, cover, and simmer very gently for 15 to 20 minutes until the chicken is no longer pink in the middle. Transfer the chicken to a warm platter and cover loosely with foil to keep warm. Pour the evaporated milk into the pan and add the cornstarch mixture. Bring to a boil and reduce heat to a simmer. Return the chicken to the pan and turn to coat with the sauce. Gently stir in the halved grapes. Serve immediately.

Calories 227
Protein 22 g
Carbohydrate 10 g
Fat 10 g

Food group servings:
Protein 3
Fat 2

CHICKEN ENCHILADAS

(Makes 8 servings)

It's somewhat of an oxymoron to mention the words "light" and "Mexican food" in the same sentence, but it can be done. Traditionally, enchiladas are full of unhealthy fat and loaded with calories. Not any more. These enchiladas are scrumptious and lean, with only 7 grams of fat per serving.

8 corn tortillas

For the filling:

3 cups chicken broth

4 boneless, skinless chicken breasts

1 bay leaf

2 cloves garlic, smashed with the side of a knife

2 sprigs fresh oregano

1 small onion, quartered

¼ cup tomato paste

2 teaspoons chili powder

2 teaspoons ground cumin

Salt, to taste

For the sauce:

2 cups tomato sauce

Hot cayenne pepper sauce, to taste

¼ teaspoon ground cinnamon

1 teaspoon chili powder

1 cup low-fat shredded Cheddar cheese

Preheat the oven to 350°.

Wrap corn tortillas in foil and warm in the oven. In a large sauté pan, bring broth to a simmer and set chicken into broth with bay leaf, garlic, oregano, and onion. Cover pan and poach chicken in broth 10 minutes.

In a large saucepan combine tomato sauce, hot sauce, cinnamon, and chili powder and heat through, keeping warm until needed.

Remove chicken to a bowl and shred with 2 forks. Add ½ cup of cooking liquid, tomato paste, spices, and salt and work through the chicken using the forks.

Remove tortillas from oven and pile chicken mixture in a line down the center of the tortillas and roll. Line casserole or baking dish with enchiladas, seam side down. Pour hot tomato sauce over the enchiladas and top with cheese. Place enchiladas in hot oven and bake for 10 minutes to melt cheese and heat through.

TAMALE PIE

(Makes 8 servings)

This classic casserole has been updated to reflect a healthy lifestyle. You'll get no arguments from your kids when you serve this hearty dish. It will take more than an hour to prepare and cook, however, so you'll want to make it on a day when you can start dinner early.

Calories 363
Protein 16 g
Carbohydrate 61 g
Fat 7 g

Food group servings:
Grain 1
Vegetable 1
Protein 1.5
Fat 0.8

Nonstick cooking spray
1 medium onion, chopped
1 clove garlic, minced
3 tablespoons Smart Balance Buttery Spread
2 boneless, skinless chicken breasts, cubed
1 (16-ounce) can stewed tomatoes
1 (8-ounce) can tomato sauce
½ cup chicken broth
1½ teaspoons salt, divided
1½ to 3 tablespoons chili powder
1 teaspoon dried oregano
1 (4-ounce) can chopped green chilies
1 (12-ounce) can corn with peppers, undrained
2 cups cornmeal
4 cups water
1 cup grated nonfat Cheddar cheese

Preheat the oven to 375°.

Spray a 9½ x 13-inch casserole dish with nonstick cooking spray and set aside. In a large nonstick skillet sauté the onions and garlic in the Smart Balance until the onion is tender. Add the chicken, stewed tomatoes, tomato sauce, chicken broth, and ½ teaspoon salt. Bring to a boil, reduce heat and simmer, covered, for 30 minutes. Add the chili powder, oregano, and green chilies. Stir in the corn and simmer for 5 minutes.

In a medium saucepan, combine the cornmeal with 4 cups water and 1 teaspoon salt. Bring to a boil, whisking constantly until thickened. Remove from heat and let stand for 5 minutes. Spread the cornmeal mixture on the bottom of the casserole dish and top with the chicken mixture. Sprinkle with grated cheese. Bake uncovered for 30 minutes or until hot and the cheese has melted.

Calories 346
Protein 23 g
Carbohydrate 61 g
Fat 6 g

Food group servings:
Grain 2.8
Vegetable 0.8
Protein 3.2
Fat 1.3

CHICKEN POT PIE

(Makes 6 servings)

Chicken Pot Pie is so homey and comforting, and it's everything you need in one dish. Serve with a side salad and you've got a complete meal.

Nonstick cooking spray
1   cup chicken broth
3   carrots, cut into ½-inch chunks
1   all-purpose potato, peeled and cut into ½-inch chunks
1   parsnip, cut into ½-inch chunks
½   teaspoon salt
1   cup frozen pearl onions
1   cup frozen peas

1   pound boneless, skinless chicken breasts, cut into 2-inch pieces
½   cup evaporated skim milk
¼   cup all-purpose flour
½   teaspoon dried sage
¼   teaspoon black pepper
2   17 x 11-inch sheets phyllo dough, cut crosswise into halves

Preheat the oven to 375°. Spray a 9-inch deep-dish pie plate with non-stick cooking spray.

In a large saucepan, combine the broth, carrots, potato, parsnip, and ¼ teaspoon of the salt. Bring to a boil over high heat, reduce to a simmer, cover, and cook until the potato is almost tender, about 5 minutes. Stir in the pearl onions, peas, and chicken and return to a boil. Then reduce to a simmer and cover and cook until the chicken is cooked through, about 5 minutes.

In another large saucepan, combine the evaporated skim milk, flour, sage, remaining ¼ teaspoon salt, and pepper. Bring to a boil, reduce to a simmer, and cook until the sauce is thickened to the consistency of heavy cream, about 2 minutes. Stir in the chicken mixture and cook for 1 minute longer.

Spoon the chicken mixture into a 9-inch deep-dish pie pan. Layer the phyllo sheets on top, overlapping the sheets at right angles, tucking in the edges and lightly spraying the corners with nonstick spray.

Bake the pot pie for 10 to 15 minutes, or until the filling is heated through and the phyllo is crisp and golden. Serve immediately.

SESAME GINGER CHICKEN

(Makes 6 servings)

Calories 509
Protein 27 g
Carbohydrate 78 g
Fat 11 g

Food group servings:
Grain 2
Vegetable 1.6
Fruit 0.5
Fat 2.2
Protein 3.8

I know this recipe has a lot of ingredients and some of them may seem a bit esoteric, but the good news is that this recipe is actually simple to make and you should be able to find all of the ingredients in your local grocery store. Your kids will love the idea of having Chinese take-out-style food at home—and it makes a full meal, all in one.

2 tablespoons olive oil	½ cup finely chopped celery
6 boneless, skinless chicken breasts	½ cup finely chopped green onions
½ cup orange juice	1 (8-ounce) can sliced water chestnuts, drained
3 tablespoons tamari or reduced-sodium soy sauce	½ pound snow peas
6 tablespoons rice vinegar	1 (11-ounce) can mandarin oranges
3 tablespoons honey	4 cups shredded Napa cabbage
1 teaspoon dark sesame oil	6 cups cooked brown rice
½ teaspoon ground ginger	1 tablespoon sesame seeds
¼ teaspoon red pepper flakes	
1 red bell pepper, cut into thin strips	

In a large skillet, heat the oil over medium-high heat. Lightly brown the chicken on each side. Remove from the pan and slice into ¼-inch strips. Add the orange juice, tamari, rice vinegar, honey, sesame oil, ginger, and red pepper flakes to the pan. Cook over medium-high heat for 2 minutes.

Return the chicken to the pan along with red bell pepper, celery, green onions, water chestnuts, snow peas, and mandarin oranges, and cook for 2 minutes more, until the chicken is just cooked through. Stir to combine. Mound the cabbage on a serving platter or individual plates, mound the rice on top (1 cup of rice per serving), and pour the chicken mixture over all. Garnish with the sesame seeds.

FRUIT-GLAZED PORK TENDERLOIN

(Makes 8 servings)

If you've never had pork tenderloin, give this recipe a try. It's incredibly tender and as long as you don't overcook it, incredibly moist. The glaze on this pork tenderloin gets sticky and sweet and really adds great flavor.

4	(12-ounce) pork tenderloins	½	teaspoon ground cinnamon
1¼	teaspoons salt	1	tablespoon plus 1½ teaspoons
½	teaspoon black pepper		balsamic vinegar
	Nonstick cooking spray	1	garlic clove, minced
⅓	cup orange marmalade	3	tablespoons liquid Butter Buds
⅓	cup apricot jam	6	cups mixed salad greens

Preheat the oven to 400°.

Season tenderloins with salt and pepper. Spray a large nonstick skillet with nonstick cooking spray and place over medium-high heat. Brown the pork on all sides and transfer to a foil-lined baking sheet and place in the oven for 10 minutes.

Meanwhile, in a small bowl, whisk together orange marmalade, apricot jam, and cinnamon. Transfer 1 tablespoon of the jam mixture to a large bowl and set aside. Brush the pork with the remaining jam mixture and bake for 10 to 15 minutes more, until a meat thermometer registers 160°. Let the pork stand for 5 minutes before slicing into 1-inch slices.

Whisk the vinegar, garlic, and Butter Buds into the reserved jam mixture. Add the greens and toss to coat. Serve the sliced pork on top of the mixed greens.

JAMBALAYA

(Makes 8 servings)

This may not be authentically Cajun, but it's authentically delicious and so easy to prepare.

Calories 266
Protein 35 g
Carbohydrate 16 g
Fat 7 g

Food group servings:
Vegetable 1.4
Protein 5
Fat 0.6

2	medium onions, chopped		Cayenne pepper, to taste
2	garlic cloves, minced	½	teaspoon dried thyme
2	tablespoons Smart Balance Bottled Oil	1	teaspoon Worcestershire sauce
1	(16-ounce) can diced tomatoes	⅛	teaspoon ground cloves
1	(6-ounce) can tomato paste	1	pound lump crabmeat, checked for bits of shell
2	stalks celery, chopped		
1	green bell pepper, chopped	2	cups water
	Salt and pepper, to taste	1	cup rice
		2	pounds cooked large shrimp

In a large nonstick skillet, sauté the onions and garlic in the oil until soft, about 5 minutes. Add the tomatoes, tomato paste, celery, bell pepper, salt and pepper, cayenne pepper, thyme, Worcestershire sauce, and cloves. Simmer, uncovered, for 20 minutes, stirring occasionally. Stir in the crabmeat and the water and bring to a boil. Add the rice and continue to simmer until rice is tender, about 15 minutes. Stir in the cooked shrimp at the last minute, just to warm through, and serve immediately.

SWEET-SPICY GLAZED SALMON

(Makes 4 servings)

Calories 290
Protein 37 g
Carbohydrate 11 g
Fat 10 g

Food group servings:
Protein 5
Fat 2

If you have trouble getting your kids to eat fish, this may just be the recipe that does the trick. Like the title promises, it's sweet, it's slightly spicy, and it's incredibly easy to make for a busy weeknight dinner.

3	tablespoons dark brown sugar	4	(6-ounce) salmon fillets
1	tablespoon low-sodium soy sauce		Nonstick cooking spray
4	teaspoons Chinese-style mustard	¼	teaspoon salt
1	teaspoon unseasoned rice vinegar	¼	teaspoon black pepper

Preheat the oven to 425°.

In a small saucepan over medium heat combine the brown sugar, soy sauce, Chinese mustard, and rice vinegar and bring to a boil. Remove from heat.

Meanwhile, place salmon on a foil-lined baking pan sprayed with nonstick spray. Season the salmon with salt and pepper. Bake for 12 minutes. Remove from oven.

Preheat the broiler.

Brush the sugar mixture evenly over the salmon and broil 3 inches from the heat to caramelize the glaze. Serve immediately.

FISH STICKS WITH RANCH DIPPING SAUCE

(Makes 6 servings)

Calories 353
Protein 29 g
Carbohydrate 27 g
Fat 14 g

Food group servings:
Grain 1
Milk/Yogurt 0.1
Protein 4
Fat 2.6

Baked instead of fried, these fish sticks are just as crunchy and just as delicious. Kids love to help out with the breading, which means lots of fun for them, less work for you.

Nonstick cooking spray	½ teaspoon dry mustard, divided
1½ pounds fresh cod fillets	¼ teaspoon black pepper
⅔ cup nonfat milk	¼ cup Smart Balance Buttery
⅔ cup all-purpose flour	Spread, melted
1 cup plain dry bread crumbs	⅓ cup nonfat sour cream
1 (1-ounce) envelope ranch dress-	⅓ cup light mayonnaise
ing mix, divided	2 to 3 tablespoons nonfat milk

Preheat the oven to 450°.

Lightly coat a baking sheet with nonstick cooking spray. Set aside.

Wash the fish fillets and pat them dry with paper towels. Cut the fish into 3 x 1-inch strips. Meanwhile, pour the milk into one shallow dish and place the flour in another shallow dish. In a third shallow dish, combine the bread crumbs and 2 tablespoons of the ranch dressing mix, ¼ teaspoon of the mustard, and the pepper. Add the melted Smart Balance and stir with a fork to combine and break up any clumps.

Dip the fish into the milk, then into the flour, being careful to shake off the excess, and then into the bread crumb mixture, coating well. Place the fish on the prepared cookie sheet and bake 10 to 12 minutes until golden brown and firm to the touch.

Meanwhile, for the dipping sauce, in a small bowl combine the sour cream, mayonnaise, remaining ¼ teaspoon of dry mustard, and remaining ranch dressing mix along with 2 to 3 tablespoons of the milk to achieve desired consistency. Serve the sauce beside the fish sticks.

Calories 299
Protein 30 g
Carbohydrate 33 g
Fat 4 g

Food group servings:
Grain 2
Protein 4
Fat 1

SHRIMP AND CORN WRAPS

(Makes 4 servings)

These Shrimp and Corn Wraps are so good you'll find yourself looking for reasons to make them.

1	pound peeled and deveined shrimp	1	stalk celery, finely chopped
3	tablespoons liquid Butter Buds	1	tablespoon fresh lemon juice
	Salt and pepper, to taste	1	garlic clove, minced
	Nonstick cooking spray	⅓	cup nonfat mayonnaise
1	cup corn kernels, canned or frozen	½	teaspoon paprika
		½	teaspoon cayenne pepper
4	(10-inch) low-fat whole-wheat tortillas	1½	cups shredded Napa cabbage

Preheat the oven to 400°.

In a medium bowl toss the shrimp with Butter Buds and season with salt and pepper. Place the shrimp in a single layer on a baking sheet sprayed with nonstick cooking spray and cook in the oven for 8 to 12 minutes, until pink, curled, and firm to the touch. Transfer to a plate. Heat corn in the microwave or on the stove top (drain corn, if using canned corn).

Meanwhile, wrap the tortillas in foil and place in the oven to warm through. Transfer the corn to a bowl to cool slightly, then stir in the celery, lemon juice, garlic, mayonnaise, paprika, cayenne pepper, and then the cabbage. Mound the cabbage mixture in the center of each tortilla, top with shrimp and roll up. Cut into halves and serve immediately.

SHRIMP SCAMPI

(Makes 10 servings)

This is a special dish fit for entertaining. Shrimp scampi is typically swimming in melted butter (no pun intended). This version has all the butter flavor with none of the fat. Served over a mound of steaming rice and showered with fresh chopped parsley, it makes a dramatic and beautiful presentation. (For more fiber and nutrients, choose brown rice rather than white rice.)

Calories 299
Protein 28 g
Carbohydrate 38 g
Fat 3 g

Food group servings:
Grain 1
Protein 3.2
Fat 0.6

	Nonstick cooking spray	¼	cup chopped fresh parsley, divided
½	cup liquid Butter Buds		
½	teaspoon salt	2	pounds peeled and deveined raw shrimp
6	garlic cloves, minced or pressed		
2	teaspoons grated lemon zest	4	cups cooked white or brown rice
2	tablespoons lemon juice	1	lemon, cut into 6 wedges

Preheat the oven to 400°.

Spray a 13 x 9 x 2-inch baking dish with nonstick cooking spray and set aside. In a medium bowl, combine the Butter Buds, salt, garlic, lemon zest, lemon juice, and 2 tablespoons of the parsley. Toss the shrimp with the Butter Buds mixture and spread shrimp in a single layer in the prepared casserole dish. Set the baking dish aside (you'll use the liquid later). Bake uncovered for 10 to 12 minutes, until pink and just tender. Mound the rice on a serving platter and arrange the shrimp over the top. Pour the Butter Buds mixture over the top of the dish and sprinkle with remaining parsley. Garnish with lemon wedges and serve immediately.

USING FRUIT ZEST

Zest refers to the finely grated or chopped peel of a piece of citrus. The pith (the white part underneath) is bitter, so avoid that! All the intense flavor is in the zest because of the essential oils, whose flavor is even more intense than that of the juice itself. You can use a rasp (or zester, available in kitchen stores) or the small holes of an ordinary cheese grater to gently grate peel of the fruit.

TROPICAL SHRIMP SKEWERS

(Makes 4 servings)

Your kids will love taking a virtual trip to the islands with these Tropical Shrimp Skewers.

Nonstick cooking spray

12 ounces medium peeled and deveined shrimp

½ small peeled, cored fresh pineapple, sliced ½ inch thick and quartered

½ teaspoon lemon pepper seasoning

3 tablespoons Poppy Seed Dressing (see page 169)

1 tablespoon pineapple juice

Preheat the broiler.

Spray a baking sheet with nonstick cooking spray and set aside. Alternately thread the shrimp and pineapple onto bamboo skewers and sprinkle with lemon pepper seasoning. Place the shrimp skewers on baking pan and broil for 4 minutes.

Meanwhile, in a small bowl combine the Poppy Seed Dressing and pineapple juice and brush both sides of the shrimp skewers. Broil for 3 to 4 minutes more until shrimp are opaque and curled. Serve immediately.

BOSTON BAKED BEANS

(Makes 8 servings)

Boston baked beans conjure up memories of cookouts and potlucks on warm summer nights. But don't wait until summer to make these beans. These are so good you'll want to enjoy them any time of the year.

Calories 184
Protein 7 g
Carbohydrate 28 g
Fat 5 g

Food group servings:
Vegetable 0.5
Protein 1
Fat 1

2	cups dried white or navy beans	1	teaspoon salt
6	slices turkey bacon, diced	1/8	teaspoon black pepper
2	medium onions, finely chopped	1/2	teaspoon dried mustard
1/3	cup light brown sugar	1/4	cup chili sauce
3	tablespoons molasses		

Preheat the oven to 300°.

Cook the beans according to package directions until tender (you can cook them in a slow cooker if you prefer). Reserve 2 cups of their cooking liquid.

Cook the bacon and onions until the onions are soft, about 5 minutes. Add to the beans and stir to combine. Add the brown sugar, molasses, salt, pepper, dried mustard, and chili sauce. Combine thoroughly and pour into a casserole dish. Cover with aluminum foil and bake for 2 hours. Remove the foil and bake for 1/2 hour more until the top begins to form a crust. Serve hot.

Calories 396
Protein 12.7 g
Carbohydrate 72.7 g
Fat 6.7 g

Food group servings:
Grain 3
Vegetable 0.75
Fat 1.3

INDIAN VEGETABLE CURRY

(Makes 8 servings)

There's nothing like a little culinary globetrotting to inject some life into an otherwise dull week. The exotic flavors in this curry dish will open your children's eyes to a whole new flavor experience.

2   to 3 teaspoons curry powder
1   (16-ounce) can potatoes, sliced and drained
1   (16-ounce) bag frozen vegetable medley (broccoli, cauliflower, and carrots)
1   (15-ounce) can chick-peas, drained

1   (14.5-ounce) can stewed tomatoes
1   (13¾-ounce) can vegetable broth
2   tablespoons cornstarch
6   cups cooked white or brown rice

Cook the curry powder in a large nonstick skillet, stirring constantly, over high heat until fragrant, about 30 seconds. Stir in the potatoes, vegetables, chick-peas, and tomatoes. Bring the mixture to a boil and reduce heat to medium-high. Cover and cook 8 minutes.

In a small bowl, blend vegetable broth with cornstarch and stir into vegetables. Bring to a boil and stir until thickened, about 30 seconds. Serve over rice.

VEGETARIAN

SPAGHETTI SQUASH PRIMAVERA

(Makes 4 servings)

Calories 162
Protein 6 g
Carbohydrate 32 g
Fat 3 g

Food group servings:
Grain 0.25
Vegetable 3.25
Fat 0.6

Spaghetti squash holds a special fascination for kids because of its unique ability to form spaghetti-like strands once it's cooked. Children will be curious to try it for that reason alone—and they'll keep eating because it's delicious. This is a great multitasking recipe because you can make the sauce while the squash is microwaving and cooling enough to handle. It's also great topped with Alfredo Sauce (see page 124) and garnished with a few chopped tomatoes and torn fresh basil leaves.

1	spaghetti squash (about 2 pounds)	½	cup thinly sliced yellow squash
2	tablespoons liquid Butter Buds	½	cup thinly sliced zucchini
1	garlic clove, minced	½	cup corn kernels
¼	cup chopped red onion	½	teaspoon dried oregano leaves
¼	cup thinly sliced carrot	⅛	teaspoon dried thyme leaves
¼	cup thinly sliced red bell pepper	4	teaspoons grated Parmesan cheese, for garnish
¼	cup thinly sliced green bell pepper	2	tablespoons finely chopped fresh parsley, for garnish
1	(14.5-ounce) can Italian-style stewed tomatoes		

Cut the spaghetti squash lengthwise into halves. Scoop out the seeds and pulp. Cover the halves with plastic wrap and microwave on high for 9 minutes or until the squash is soft and the strands separate easily with a fork.

Meanwhile, heat the Butter Buds in a large nonstick pan over medium-high heat. Add the garlic, onion, carrot, and peppers. Cook for 5 minutes until soft. Add tomatoes, yellow squash, zucchini, corn, oregano, and thyme. Cook for 5 minutes more until soft.

Divide "spaghetti" strands evenly among 4 plates. Spoon vegetables over the spaghetti and sprinkle with cheese and parsley. Serve immediately.

Slow Cooker Meals

A busy parent's best friend can be the slow cooker, or Crock Pot. Just pop the ingredients in your cooker ahead of time, and hours later you'll have a steaming hot, healthy, and delicious meal.

BEEF AND MUSHROOM GRAVY WITH POTATOES
(Makes 6 servings)

This is the ultimate meat and potatoes meal. It's so big on flavor that your meat and potato eaters will never know it's also low in fat.

Nonstick cooking spray

2 pounds of beef eye of round, cut into ½-inch pieces, all visible fat removed

1 cup nonfat onion-flavored beef broth

1 envelope dry onion soup mix

1 (10¾-ounce) can 98% nonfat cream of mushroom soup

1 (8-ounce) package sliced fresh mushrooms

7 medium potatoes, washed

Spray a slow cooker with nonstick cooking spray. In the cooker stir together the beef, beef broth, onion soup mix, mushroom soup, and mushrooms until well mixed. Put potatoes on top. Cover and cook on high for 5 hours. To serve, cut the potatoes into halves lengthwise and spoon 1 cup beef and mushroom gravy over them.

Calories 327
Protein 20 g
Carbohydrate 42 g
Fat 9 g

Food group servings:
Grain 2.3
Protein 2.5
Fat 1.8

BEEF ROAST EXCELLENTE

(Makes 6 servings)

It may sound weird to cook beef roast in soda pop, but trust me on this one. The ginger ale reduces and forms a sticky, sweet glaze. Once you cook a roast this way, you simply won't cook it any other way.

Calories 302
Protein 18 g
Carbohydrate 47 g
Fat 5 g

Food group servings:
Grain 2
Protein 2.5
Fat 1

Nonstick cooking spray
2   pounds eye of round roast, all visible fat removed
    Salt and pepper, to taste
4   cups ginger ale (not diet)

1   tablespoon minced garlic
6   medium potatoes
3   large onions, cut into quarters

Spray a slow cooker with nonstick cooking spray. Place the roast in the slow cooker and season with salt and pepper. Pour the ginger ale over the roast. Stir in the garlic. Place the potatoes and onions on top of the roast. Cover and cook on low for 7 to 9 hours or on high for 3½ to 4 hours.

TARRAGON CHICKEN AND POTATOES

(Makes 4 servings)

Calories 277
Protein 22 g
Carbohydrate 40 g
Fat 3 g

Food group servings:
Grain 2
Protein 4
Fat 0.6

There is something so French about the pairing of chicken and tarragon. But that's where any similarity to French food ends. This dish is decidedly American and decidedly easy to prepare.

Nonstick cooking spray

4 boneless, skinless chicken breasts

1 teaspoon dried tarragon

1 garlic clove, minced

4 tablespoons Butter Buds granules, divided

Salt and pepper, to taste

5 large red skinned potatoes

Spray a slow cooker with nonstick cooking spray. Rub the chicken with the dried tarragon, garlic, 2 tablespoons of the Butter Buds sprinkles, and salt and pepper. Place the chicken in a slow cooker. Place the potatoes on top of the chicken. Sprinkle the potatoes with the remaining 2 tablespoons of Butter Buds and salt and pepper. Cover and cook on low for 8 to 10 hours or on high for 4 to 5 hours.

CHICKEN STROGANOFF

(Makes 6 servings)

Calories 234
Protein 22 g
Carbohydrate 29 g
Fat 3 g

Food group servings:
Grain 1.3
Vegetable 0.5
Protein 2.5
Fat 0.6

Just as good as the beef stroganoff, and a bit lighter.

Nonstick cooking spray
1 pound boneless, skinless chicken breast, cut into ½-inch cubes
1 onion, chopped
8 ounces sliced mushrooms
2 garlic cloves, minced
3 cups chicken broth
4 cups medium-size yolk-free egg noodles
1 cup nonfat sour cream

Spray the slow cooker with nonstick cooking spray. In the cooker combine the chicken, onions, mushrooms, garlic, and chicken broth and mix well. Cover and cook on low for 4 to 6 hours or on high for 2 to 3 hours. (If cooking on low, turn the temperature to high before stirring in the noodles.) Stir in the noodles, cover, and cook for another 30 minutes or until the noodles are cooked. Stir in the sour cream and serve.

CINNAMON CHICKEN

(Makes 4 servings)

Can't help but be intrigued by the idea of chicken gently perfumed with cinnamon and orange zest? Cinnamon is quite a common ingredient in savory foods in Middle Eastern cooking, and the flavor is surprisingly delicious. The key is to use only a hint of cinnamon—otherwise you're treading dangerously close to apple pie territory.

	Nonstick cooking spray	1	teaspoon fresh orange zest
½	teaspoon ground cinnamon	1	pound boneless, skinless
1	tablespoon dark brown sugar		chicken breasts, cut into
½	cup nonfat red wine vinegar		½ x 4-inch-long strips
	dressing		

Spray a slow cooker with nonstick cooking spray. In a small bowl mix together the cinnamon, brown sugar, vinegar dressing, and orange zest. Place the chicken in the slow cooker and cover with the dressing mixture. Cover and cook on high for 3 to 4 hours or on low for 6 to 8 hours.

LEMON PEPPER PORK TENDERLOIN WITH LEMON-KISSED POTATOES

(Makes 8 servings)

Calories 323
Protein 34 g
Carbohydrate 30 g
Fat 7 g

Food group servings:
Grain 2
Protein 4
Fat 1.4

This dish is good enough for company. The pork tenderloin is spiked with lemon and garlic and the potatoes (as the title promises) are ever so gently kissed with the fragrance of lemon.

	Nonstick cooking spray	1	teaspoon garlic salt
2	pounds pork tenderloin, all visible fat removed	8	medium potatoes, diced into ½-inch cubes
2	medium lemons, cut into quarters, seeds discarded	1	cup water
		1	teaspoon cream of tartar
1	teaspoon black pepper	1	teaspoon dried parsley

Spray a slow cooker with nonstick cooking spray. With a knife, cut the pork tenderloin down the center lengthwise to divide in half. Cut ¼-inch deep cuts all over the pork. Squeeze the lemon juice onto the tenderloin and sprinkle it lightly with the pepper and garlic salt. Place the meat in the slow cooker. Place the diced potatoes in a bowl with the water and cream of tartar, and let them soak for 1 minute. (This will keep the potatoes from getting discolored while cooking.) Then place the potatoes on top of the meat in the slow cooker and sprinkle with the parsley. Arrange any remaining lemon quarters on top. Cook on high for 2½ to 3 hours or on low for 6 to 8 hours. Remove lemons before serving.

Calories 196
Protein 20 g
Carbohydrate 23 g
Fat 3 g

Food group servings:
Grain 1.5
Protein 1
Fat 0.6

PIZZA PASTA

(Makes 4 servings)

All the flavors of pizza over pasta. And I don't have to tell you that this has far fewer calories and a fraction of the fat of your local delivery pizza.

Nonstick cooking spray

2   cups hot water

1   (14-ounce) jar pizza sauce

½   cup chopped onion

2   ounces reduced-fat turkey pepperoni, cut into thin strips

8   ounces sliced fresh mushrooms

1½ cups elbow macaroni

¼   cup low-fat shredded mozzarella cheese

Spray a slow cooker with nonstick spray. In the slow cooker stir together the water, pizza sauce, onion, pepperoni, and mushrooms. Cover and cook on high for 1 hour. Add the macaroni and cook for ½ hour more. Sprinkle with the cheese. Cover and cook on high for another 10 minutes or until the cheese melts.

SLOW-COOKED COWBOY BEANS

(Makes 8 servings)

Calories 358
Protein 24 g
Carbohydrate 50 g
Fat 8 g

Food group servings:
Vegetable 0.5
Protein 3.4
Fat 1.6

The title alone suggests a romanticized life on the range, evenings spent huddled around a glowing campfire, slowly stirring a pot of "grub." Maybe this is a dish that cowboys ate after a long hard day. Whether they did or not, your children will love the notion.

1 pound ground turkey breast	¾ cup brown sugar
1 (16-ounce) can baked beans, undrained	1 cup ketchup
1 (16-ounce) can kidney beans, drained	2 tablespoons dry mustard
2 cups chopped onions	¼ teaspoon salt
	2 teaspoons cider vinegar

Brown the turkey in a nonstick skillet over medium heat. In a slow cooker, combine the turkey, baked beans, kidney beans, onions, brown sugar, ketchup, dry mustard, salt, and cider vinegar and stir to combine. Cover and cook on high for 1 to 2 hours.

Pasta, Noodles, and Sauces

Need I mention that kids love pasta and noodles—and that these foods are fast and easy to prepare? Here are some delicious dishes, including several kids' classics, and marvelous sauces that will go well with any type of pasta or noodles. (It's best to choose whole-wheat pasta and yolk-free noodles.)

QUICK SLOPPY JOE CASSEROLE
(Makes 9 servings)

You already know that your kids love Sloppy Joes, but the operative word here is "quick." This is perfect for a busy school night when you're pressed for time. You can make this ahead and store in the refrigerator covered tightly for up to two days.

Calories 141
Protein 16 g
Carbohydrate 13 g
Fat 3 g

Food group servings:
Grain 0.5
Protein 2
Fat 0.6

Nonstick cooking spray
1 (8-ounce) package shell macaroni
½ pound ground turkey breast
1 envelope Sloppy Joe mix
1 (6-ounce) can tomato paste
1 (8-ounce) can tomato sauce

1 cup water
1 (16-ounce) carton nonfat cottage cheese or nonfat ricotta cheese
1 cup grated nonfat Cheddar cheese

Preheat the oven to 375°.

Spray a casserole dish with nonstick spray and set aside. Fill a large stockpot with water; bring it to a boil, and cook the shells as the package directs. Meanwhile, cook the ground turkey in a medium skillet over medium-high heat. Add the Sloppy Joe mix, tomato paste, tomato sauce, and water. Cook until thickened, about 2 minutes. Layer half the macaroni in the casserole dish, along with half the cottage cheese and half the meat sauce. Repeat the layers one more time and top with Cheddar cheese. Bake, uncovered, for 40 to 50 minutes.

GIANT SHELL LASAGNA

(Makes 8 servings)

Calories 388
Protein 46 g
Carbohydrate 32 g
Fat 8 g

Food group servings:
Grain 1
Protein 6
Fat 1.6

This recipe has all of the flavors and textures of traditional lasagna with half the work and way less than half the fat. The recipe makes two casseroles: You can make them ahead of time and store them covered in the refrigerator for up to two days, or you can freeze one for another day.

1 (12-ounce) package giant shells Nonstick cooking spray	1 (15-ounce) carton nonfat ricotta cheese
1 pound ground turkey breast, cooked and drained	¾ cup egg substitute, beaten
	½ cup nonfat Parmesan cheese
2 (26¾-ounce) cans Hunts Light Spaghetti Sauce	3 cups grated nonfat mozzarella cheese

Preheat the oven to 350°.

Cook the shells according to package directions; drain, rinse and drain again.

Spray two 9-inch square casserole dishes with nonstick cooking spray and set aside. (If you don't have dishes in these sizes, use whatever you have.) Cook the turkey in a bowl in the microwave, covered with a piece of waxed paper, for about 5 minutes. Remove and stir, and cook for 3 to 4 more minutes. Drain the turkey and combine with the spaghetti sauce in a large bowl.

In another medium bowl, combine the ricotta cheese, egg substitute, and 4 tablespoons of Parmesan cheese. Pour a little of the sauce into the bottom of each casserole dish and spread the ricotta cheese mixture over the sauce. Layer in the giant shells and then sprinkle half of the remaining Parmesan cheese on top of each dish. Repeat layers with sauce and giant shells, and end with mozzarella cheese and Parmesan cheese sprinkled on top. Bake for 30 to 40 minutes. This casserole can also be cooked in the microwave for 10 minutes and browned in the oven for 5 to 8 minutes.

CHICKEN CACCIATORE

(Makes 4 servings)

Calories 192
Protein 23 g
Carbohydrate 12 g
Fat 4 g

Food group servings:
Vegetable 1.5
Protein 3.4
Fat 0.8

Another one of those "Italian grandma favorites" that needed a little lightening up. This will make her proud. (You can substitute chicken broth for the white wine if desired.)

Nonstick cooking spray
4 boneless, skinless chicken breasts
1 onion, chopped
2 garlic cloves, minced
1 (16-ounce) can Italian tomatoes
1 cup tomato sauce
½ cup white wine (the alcohol cooks out)
¼ teaspoon basil
¼ teaspoon oregano
1 bay leaf
½ teaspoon salt
1 cup sliced mushrooms

Spray a large nonstick skillet with nonstick cooking spray and brown the chicken, onion, and garlic. Add tomatoes, tomato sauce, wine, basil, oregano, bay leaf, and salt. Bring to a boil, then cover and gently simmer for 30 minutes. Add mushrooms and cook for 10 minutes more. Remove the chicken from the pan and reduce sauce until thickened, about 5 minutes. Serve over pasta.

HOW TO COOK PERFECT PASTA

- Use plenty of water (at least 4 quarts per pound of pasta) to keep it from sticking together.
- Add salt to the water (about 1 tablespoon of salt per pound of pasta).
- When the water is boiling, add the pasta gradually, stirring while you do.
- If the pasta doesn't fit in the pot, use a spoon to bend it as it cooks.
- Stir it occasionally to prevent sticking, and don't cover the pot.
- Check frequently, especially if you are cooking it al dente (still firm when you bite it).
- Drain pasta in a colander.
- Enjoy!

CHICKEN TETRAZZINI

(Makes 8 servings)

This retro dish with great appeal seems to have vanished from the culinary terrain. I say it's time for a reissue. Your kids will thank you.

Calories 223
Protein 28 g
Carbohydrate 16 g
Fat 4 g

Food group servings:
Grain 0.3
Vegetable 0.1
Milk/Yogurt 0.1
Protein 3
Fat 0.8

Nonstick cooking spray
- 1/4 cup liquid Butter Buds
- 1/4 cup all-purpose flour
- 1/2 teaspoon salt
- 1/4 teaspoon black pepper
- 1 cup chicken broth
- 1 cup evaporated skim milk
- 2 tablespoons dry sherry
- 2 cups cooked, cubed skinless chicken breasts
- 1 (8-ounce) can mushrooms
- 1 (7-ounce) package spaghetti, cooked al dente
- 1/4 cup Parmesan cheese
- 1 cup grated nonfat mozzarella cheese

Preheat the oven to 350°.

Spray a 9½ x 11-inch casserole dish with nonstick cooking spray. In a medium saucepan over medium heat, whisk together the Butter Buds, flour, salt, and pepper and cook until bubbly. Whisk in the chicken broth and evaporated skim milk and heat to boiling, stirring constantly for one minute. Stir in the sherry, chicken, and mushrooms; pour the sauce over the spaghetti and stir to combine. Pour into the prepared casserole dish, top with the Parmesan and mozzarella cheese, and bake uncovered for 30 minutes, until bubbly. To brown the top, place briefly under the broiler. Serve immediately.

TUNA NOODLE CASSEROLE

(Makes 6 servings)

There's something comforting about casseroles, but no one seems to make them anymore. I think it's time to update them and bring them back into fashion, and Tuna Noodle Casserole is a sure-fire kid favorite.

Nonstick cooking spray
½ cup chopped celery
8 ounces sliced fresh mushrooms
1 teaspoon celery salt
1½ cups nonfat sour cream
2 (6-ounce) cans water-packed tuna, drained
¾ cup nonfat milk
1 teaspoon Mrs. Dash onion herb mixture
½ teaspoon white pepper
8 ounces yolk-free egg noodles, cooked al dente
¼ cup Parmesan cheese
¼ cup dry bread crumbs
¼ cup chopped fresh parsley

Preheat the oven to 350°.

Spray a nonstick skillet with nonstick cooking spray and sauté the celery and mushrooms with the celery salt until soft. In a large bowl, combine the mushroom mixture with the sour cream, tuna, milk, herb mixture, and pepper. Toss the noodles gently into the mixture.

Spray a 2-quart casserole dish with nonstick cooking spray and turn the noodle mixture into it. Mix together the Parmesan, bread crumbs, and parsley. Sprinkle over the top of the casserole and bake uncovered for 35 to 40 minutes.

CORKSCREW PASTA WITH TOMATO CREAM SAUCE

(Makes 6 servings)

Calories 289
Protein 11 g
Carbohydrate 55 g
Fat 3 g

Food group servings:
Grain 3.5
Vegetable 0.3
Milk/Yogurt 0.1
Fat 0.6

Pasta is a great standby for quick and easy meals. Topped with this low-fat creamy tomato sauce and served with a crisp green salad drizzled with low-fat dressing—violá, a complete and satisfying meal. This sauce can be frozen in individual portions in freezer bags for a quick lunch or dinner.

	Salt and pepper, to taste	⅔	cup evaporated skim milk
	Nonstick cooking spray	2	tablespoons chopped fresh
2	garlic cloves, minced or pressed		basil, oregano, and parsley
1	(14-ounce) can chopped tomatoes	1	pound corkscrew pasta

In a large stockpot heat enough boiling water to cook the pasta according to package directions. Meanwhile, spray a nonstick medium saucepan with cooking spray and sauté the garlic for 1 minute. Stir in the tomatoes and bring to a boil. Reduce heat and simmer, uncovered for 20 minutes, stirring occasionally. Stir in the evaporated skim milk and simmer for 5 more minutes to thicken sauce. Stir in the fresh herbs and the salt and pepper. Toss the sauce with the hot pasta and serve immediately.

PASTA SALAD WITH SHRIMP

(Makes 12 servings)

Everybody loves a good pasta salad. With the addition of fresh shrimp, this salad is really something special.

12 ounces corkscrew pasta	½ cup chopped bell pepper
½ cup liquid Butter Buds	1 small onion, diced
1 pint nonfat mayonnaise	½ cup chopped celery
¼ cup lemon juice	½ teaspoon salt
1 teaspoon Accent	½ teaspoon black pepper
1 teaspoon curry powder	1 pound large shrimp, cooked
2 teaspoons dill	

Cook the pasta according to package directions in a large stockpot, strain in a colander, and run under cold water to cool. Meanwhile, in a large bowl combine Butter Buds, mayonnaise, lemon juice, Accent, curry powder, dill, bell pepper, onion, celery, salt, and pepper. Toss the sauce with the pasta and stir in the shrimp. Cover and chill for 4 hours or overnight. Serve chilled.

MACARONI AND CHEESE

(Makes 4 servings)

Calories 334
Protein 21 g
Carbohydrate 46 g
Fat 7 g

Food group servings:
Grain 2.5
Milk/Yogurt 0.5
Protein 2.5
Fat 1.4

Few things in life are more comforting or satisfying than rich, creamy macaroni and cheese. And of course, few things are more fattening. But it doesn't have to be that way. This version packs all the flavor and a fraction of the fat.

2 cups nonfat milk

3 tablespoons cornstarch

1½ cups grated low-fat Cheddar cheese

2 tablespoons Smart Balance Light Buttery Spread

1 teaspoon salt

½ teaspoon black pepper

5 cups cooked elbow macaroni

Combine the milk and the cornstarch in a 2-quart microwave-safe casserole dish and cook on high for 4 minutes. Stir in the grated cheese, Smart Balance, salt, and pepper. Fold in the cooked macaroni and cook uncovered on high for 4 minutes more.

CARIBBEAN PASTA SALAD WITH TROPICAL ISLAND DRESSING

(Makes 6 servings)

Calories 338
Protein 12 g
Carbohydrate 60 g
Fat 7 g

Food group servings:
Grain 1
Vegetable 1
Milk/Yogurt 0.2
Protein 0.4
Fat 1.4

This salad is packed with so many great flavors and colors it's like a party on a plate. (If you can't find piña colada low-fat yogurt, substitute vanilla or coconut.)

For the salad:

1   (15-ounce) can black beans, drained and rinsed

½   cup thawed orange juice concentrate

½   teaspoon ground allspice

6   ounces corkscrew pasta

1   teaspoon liquid Butter Buds

4   cups washed and torn romaine lettuce leaves

1½   cups canned pineapple chunks

1   mango, peeled and sliced

1   cup shredded cabbage

⅓   cup chopped onion

⅓   cup chopped red bell pepper

2   oranges, sectioned, for garnish

For the dressing:

8   ounces piña colada-flavored low-fat yogurt

½   cup orange juice

½   teaspoon ground ginger

    Zest of 1 orange

In a medium bowl combine the beans, orange juice concentrate, and allspice. Cover and refrigerate for 1 hour.

Meanwhile, cook the pasta al dente, according to package directions. Drain. Rinse under cold water, toss with the Butter Buds, and return to the pan.

In a small bowl, combine the yogurt, ½ cup orange juice, ginger, and the zest of 1 orange. To assemble the salad, divide the lettuce, pasta, pineapple, beans, mango, cabbage, onion, and bell pepper among 6 plates. Separate the oranges into sections and arrange on top. Serve the dressing on the side.

SPAGHETTI SAUCE

(Makes 10 servings)

Calories 164
Protein 14 g
Carbohydrate 10 g
Fat 8 g

Food group servings:
Vegetable 1
Protein 1.6
Fat 1.6

I won't pretend there are only a few ingredients in this sauce or that it doesn't take a little over an hour to make. It's not hard work, mind you, just a bit of chopping, can opening, and occasional stirring. But I promise you that it tastes better than anything you can possibly get out of a jar and, like all of the sauces in this book, it can be made ahead in large quantities and stored individually in the freezer for those nights when you only have a few minutes to get dinner on the table.

	Nonstick cooking spray	1	tablespoon dried basil
1	pound lean ground beef	1	teaspoon dried oregano
1	large onion, chopped	½	teaspoon dried rosemary
4	garlic cloves, minced	1	tablespoon fresh Italian parsley
1	pound mushrooms, chopped	1	teaspoon salt
1	(28-ounce) can crushed tomatoes	1	teaspoon black pepper
1	(28-ounce) can tomato sauce	1	cup beef broth

Spray a large nonstick skillet with nonstick cooking spray and brown the ground beef along with the onion, garlic, and mushrooms. Drain off fat and put meat back in the pan. Add the tomatoes, tomato sauce, basil, oregano, rosemary, parsley, salt, pepper, and beef broth. Simmer, uncovered, for 45 minutes to an hour. Serve over whole-wheat pasta.

Calories 90
Protein 6 g
Carbohydrate 12 g
Fat 2 g

Food group servings:
Milk/Yogurt 0.2
Fat 0.4

ALFREDO SAUCE

(Makes 6 servings)

It's not the pasta that's fattening, it's the creamy sauce we drown it in. Well, don't throw out the pasta with the pasta water just yet. Instead, lighten up the sauce. Enjoy your Italian bistro favorite once again with this wonderful low-fat version.

1	cup evaporated skim milk	1	garlic clove, minced or pressed
¼	cup liquid Butter Buds	¼	teaspoon black pepper
¼	cup all-purpose flour	¼	teaspoon salt
4	teaspoons chicken broth	¼	cup Parmesan cheese

In a small saucepan over low heat combine the evaporated milk, Butter Buds, flour, and chicken broth, whisking until smooth. Add the garlic and the salt and pepper, and continue cooking and whisking until the sauce thickens, about 5 minutes. Stir in the Parmesan cheese and serve immediately over your favorite pasta.

PESTO SAUCE

(Makes 6 servings)

Calories 40
Protein 2 g
Carbohydrate 5 g
Fat 1 g

Food group servings:
Fat 0.2

This bright, fresh sauce is great for the summer, when basil is plentiful and in season. It freezes well in ice cube trays so make plenty. One word of advice: This is a raw sauce containing garlic, so a little of this sauce goes a long way.

1	bunch fresh basil	⅓	cup liquid Butter Buds
½	bunch fresh spinach or ½ (5-ounce) bag	¼	cup fresh Parmesan cheese
3	garlic cloves, chopped Zest of 1 lemon	¼	teaspoon black pepper

In the bowl of a food processor fitted with a blade, process the basil and spinach with the chopped garlic until the mixture is well chopped. Add the lemon zest and blend by setting the processor to pulse. With the food processor running, pour the liquid Butter Buds through the feed tube and process for 30 seconds to combine. Remove the top of the processor and scrape down the sides of the bowl with a rubber spatula. Add the Parmesan cheese and the pepper and process one more time to incorporate the cheese. Serve tossed with your favorite pasta.

CHAPTER 7

SOUPS AND CHILI

Soup, glorious soup. You can pack it in a thermos in your child's lunch or serve it piping hot on a weekend afternoon. Or serve with a salad and a slice of one of our delicious breads for a light dinner.

QUICK 'N' EASY SOUPS

No time to cook? Keep some canned soups in your pantry for those times when cooking isn't an option. Just check labels carefully, and opt for low-fat versions of your favorites. Serve with a slice of bread and low-fat cheese and some carrot sticks to fill up your kids.

You can also make your own soups and stews in a slow cooker—just add ingredients, put the cooker on low, and go about your day. You can toss in sliced veggies, stew meat, water, salt and pepper, and your favorite seasonings, and by dinnertime you'll have steaming hot soup, ready to serve.

TURKEY NOODLE SOUP

(Makes 5 servings)

I've never met a kid who could resist steaming hot soup on a cold winter day. This soup is packed full of moist turkey, fresh vegetables, and tender egg noodles.

Calories 252
Protein 27 g
Carbohydrate 17 g
Fat 8 g

Food group servings:
Grain 1
Vegetable 0.8
Protein 3
Fat 1.6

3 cups chicken broth	2 cups wide yolk-free egg noodles
2¼ cups water	1½ cups chopped cooked turkey or chicken
1 cup thinly sliced carrots (2 medium)	1 medium yellow summer squash, cut into cubes
1 medium onion, cut into thin wedges	2 tablespoons freshly squeezed lemon juice
½ cup thinly sliced celery (1 stalk)	
2 teaspoons fresh chopped thyme, or 1 teaspoon dried	

In a large stockpot, combine the chicken broth, water, carrots, onion, celery, and thyme (if you are using dried thyme). Bring to a boil and reduce immediately to a simmer. Cover and cook for 15 minutes.

Stir in the egg noodles, turkey, and squash. Cook, uncovered, for 8 to 10 minutes or until noodles are tender. Stir in the lemon juice and thyme (if you are using fresh thyme). Cook, uncovered, for 1 minute more.

TURKEY AND SWEET POTATO SOUP

(Makes 4 servings)

Calories 371
Protein 42 g
Carbohydrate 41 g
Fat 4 g

Food group servings:
Grain 1
Vegetable 1
Protein 4
Fat 0.8

This soup is like the flavors of Thanksgiving in a bowl. The sweet potatoes supply a certain sweetness and the sage lends a savory quality for a combination that is truly inspired. Cutting the turkey and preparing the sweet potatoes will take a while, so plan this treat for a weekend when you have some time.

2	tablespoons liquid Butter Buds
1	onion, cut into thin slices
1½	teaspoons dried sage
1	pound sweet potatoes, peeled and cut into ½-inch cubes
1½	quarts chicken broth
2	teaspoons salt
¼	teaspoon black pepper
¼	pound green beans, cut into ¼-inch pieces
1	pound white meat turkey, cut into ½-inch strips

In a large stockpot, heat the Butter Buds over medium heat, and add the onion and sage and cook until onion is translucent, about 5 minutes. Add the sweet potatoes, chicken broth, and 1 teaspoon of the salt. Bring to a boil, reduce heat, and simmer until the sweet potatoes are tender, about 10 minutes. Transfer the soup in batches to a blender and blend until smooth. Return to the stockpot over medium-high heat along with the remaining salt, pepper, green beans, and the turkey strips. Simmer just until the turkey is cooked through and the beans are tender. Serve immediately.

SPLIT PEA SOUP

(Makes 8 servings)

You may want to call this something else to get your kids to try it; use your imagination. Tell them Shrek eats it—it's the right color. Serve this up and watch it disappear.

Calories 90
Protein 7 g
Carbohydrate 12 g
Fat 2 g

Food group servings:
Grain 0.5
Protein 0.5
Fat 0.4

2	cups dried split peas	1	bay leaf
2	quarts chicken or vegetable broth	8	sprigs fresh flat-leaf parsley
1	cup chopped celery	1	medium carrot, quartered
1	medium onion, finely chopped	4	slices uncooked turkey bacon

In a large stockpot combine all the ingredients. Bring to a boil, reduce heat and simmer for 1 hour or until the peas are tender. Remove the bay leaf and the turkey bacon and discard. You can serve as is, if you like "chunky" pea soup, or you can process the soup in a blender, a cup or two at a time, until smooth.

Calories 309
Protein 23 g
Carbohydrate 46 g
Fat 7 g

Food group servings:
Grain 0.62
Vegetable 1
Protein 2
Fat 1.4

CHICKEN TORTILLA SOUP

(Makes 8 servings)

This hearty soup is not only delicious, it's incredibly easy to make. Most of these ingredients are things you probably already have on hand. The good news is, you can have it on the table in less than an hour—and it's even better reheated the next day.

1	medium onion. chopped	1½	teaspoons chili powder
1	tablespoon olive oil	1½	teaspoons cumin
2	garlic cloves, minced	2	boneless, skinless chicken breasts, cut into small strips
1	(10.5-ounce) can tomatoes with green chilies, chopped, undrained	5	corn tortillas, cut into ¼-inch strips
1	(16-ounce) can tomato sauce	8	tablespoons nonfat sour cream, for garnish
1	quart chicken broth		
1	(4-ounce) can chopped green chilies	8	ounces low-fat grated Cheddar cheese, for garnish

In a large stockpot over medium heat sauté the onion in the olive oil for 5 minutes until translucent. Add the garlic and sauté 30 seconds more. Add the tomatoes with green chilies, tomatoe sauce, chicken broth, green chilies, chili powder, and cumin. Bring to a simmer and add the chicken. Continue to simmer for 20 minutes.

Meanwhile, cut the tortillas into thin strips and add to the soup. Simmer for 15 more minutes. To serve, garnish with a tablespoon of sour cream and grated Cheddar cheese.

PENNSYLVANIA DUTCH CHICKEN CORN SOUP

(Makes 6 servings)

Calories 161
Protein 17 g
Carbohydrate 12 g
Fat 5 g

Food group servings:
Grain 0.5
Protein 2.4
Fat 1

The ingredients in this soup—corn and hard-boiled eggs—may seem like an odd combination, but the pairing works beautifully. The fresh parsley brightens up the flavor and adds a burst of freshness to canned broth. You can put this soup together in minutes, and your kids will eat it up and ask for more.

8   cups chicken broth
2   bay leaves
2   boneless, skinless chicken breast halves
1   cup corn kernels

1   cup yolk-free egg noodles
    Salt and pepper, to taste
3   hard-boiled eggs, chopped
½   cup chopped fresh flat-leaf parsley

In a large stockpot bring the chicken broth and bay leaves to a simmer. Add the chicken and poach gently just until cooked through, about 10 minutes. Remove the chicken from the pot and set aside to cool slightly. Add the corn, along with the egg noodles, and bring back to a boil. Reduce the heat and simmer gently to cook the noodles. Meanwhile, shred or chop the chicken into bite-size pieces and return to the pot. Season with salt and pepper and stir in the chopped hard-boiled egg and flat-leaf parsley. Ladle into bowls and enjoy.

Calories 131
Protein 7 g
Carbohydrate 25 g
Fat 0 g

Food group servings:
Grain 0.5
Vegetable 1
Protein 1

ITALIAN MINESTRONE SOUP

(Makes 12 servings)

If you are fortunate enough to have a doting Italian grandmother who makes big pots of soup for you, then you know how wonderful minestrone soup can be. This lighter, updated version of the old classic has all-day flavor with little of the work.

6 cups chicken broth	2 carrots, diced
½ cup dry red wine (the alcohol cooks out)	¾ pound fresh green beans, cut into thirds
1 medium onion, chopped	3 medium-size red potatoes, diced
2 stalks celery, diced	1 (16-ounce) can crushed plum tomatoes, undrained
4 garlic cloves, minced	1 cup cooked macaroni
1 bay leaf	1 (14-ounce) can cannellini beans
1 tablespoon basil	Salt and pepper, to taste
1 tablespoon oregano	

In a large stockpot bring the chicken broth and the wine to a simmer. Add the onion, celery, garlic, bay leaf, basil, oregano, carrots, green beans, and potatoes. Simmer for 30 minutes until vegetables are tender. Stir in the canned tomatoes and the macaroni, and simmer for 10 more minutes until macaroni is tender. Stir in the cannellini beans and remove and discard the bay leaf. Season with salt and pepper, to taste. Serve immediately.

VEGGIE MINESTRONE SOUP

(Makes 6 servings)

Calories 313
Protein 18 g
Carbohydrate 57 g
Fat 2 g

Food group servings:
Grain 1
Vegetable 2
Protein 2
Fat 0.4

This may be just the soup that will get your kids to eat their vegetables—and ask for more! Just a bit of Parmesan stirred in at the end gives it a wonderful, cheesy depth that kids love. Parmesan cheese is naturally low in fat, so one delicious serving of this veggie-packed soup has only 2 grams of fat.

2 quarts chicken or vegetable broth	1 (15-ounce) can diced tomatoes, undrained
2 carrots, peeled and diced	1 (10-ounce) package frozen spinach, thawed
2 medium boiling potatoes, peeled and diced	¾ cup orzo
2 small zucchini, diced	¼ teaspoon black pepper
1 cup fresh green beans, chopped into thirds	¼ cup grated Parmesan cheese
1 (15-ounce) can cannellini beans, drained and rinsed	

In a large stockpot heat the chicken broth to a simmer over medium-high heat. Add the carrots and potatoes and simmer for 10 minutes until tender. Add the zucchini, green beans, cannellini beans, tomatoes, spinach, and orzo, and bring to a boil. Simmer gently for 10 minutes, until the pasta is al dente and the vegetables are tender. Season with pepper and remove from heat. Stir in the Parmesan cheese and let stand until melted throughout.

CREAMY CORN CHOWDER

(Makes 4 servings)

Calories 275
Protein 10 g
Carbohydrate 52 g
Fat 7 g

Food group servings:
Grain 3
Vegetable 0.25
Fat 1.4

What could be better than a bowl of soul-satisfying corn chowder on a cold winter day? Because this creamy chowder is made without a lick of cream, it will provide insulation from the cold without padding your midsection.

	Nonstick cooking spray	½	teaspoon dried rosemary
1	cup chopped onion (1 medium onion)	½	teaspoon dried thyme
		⅛	teaspoon black pepper
6	cups fresh or frozen corn kernels		Cayenne pepper, to taste
3	cups chicken broth	½	tablespoon dried basil
½	cup chopped red bell pepper		

Spray the bottom of a large stockpot with the nonstick cooking spray and turn heat to medium. Sauté the onion for 5 minutes, until translucent. Add 4 cups of the corn and sauté for 5 more minutes, until it begins to soften. Pour in 2 cups of the chicken broth and bring to a simmer for 20 minutes until the corn is soft. Remove the pot from the heat and allow the soup to cool.

Carefully ladle the contents of the pan into a blender and puree in batches until smooth. Return the puree to the pan along with the bell pepper, rosemary, thyme, black pepper, cayenne pepper, basil, the remaining cup of chicken broth, and 2 cups of corn. Stir over medium heat until the chowder is thick and creamy and the corn is softened.

MYSTERY SOUP

(Makes 10 servings)

Calories 135
Protein 8 g
Carbohydrate 22 g
Fat 3 g

Food group servings:
Grain 1
Vegetable 1.5
Fat 0.2

Whatever you do, don't tell your kids this soup features broccoli and spinach! This velvety soup gets its smooth texture not from cream, but from a quick whirl in the blender. The broccoli gives it a beautiful green hue, but your kids don't have to know where the color comes from.

¼	cup Smart Balance Buttery Spread	1	pound russet potatoes, peeled and diced
4	large leeks, cleaned and chopped (white and pale green parts only)	9	cups chicken broth
1½	pounds broccoli florets, cut into pieces	1	(10-ounce) package frozen chopped spinach, undrained
		1	(7-ounce) jar roasted sweet red peppers, drained and cut into strips

In a large stockpot, heat the Smart Balance and sauté the leeks until tender but not brown, about 10 minutes. Add broccoli and potatoes and cook for 3 more minutes. Add chicken broth and bring to a boil. Reduce heat, cover and simmer until vegetables are very tender, about 20 to 25 minutes. Remove from heat and let cool to room temperature.

Add the spinach to the soup and puree in batches in a blender until smooth. Return soup to stockpot and heat gently until warmed through. To serve, top with red pepper strips.

Kids' Classic

CREAMY TOMATO SOUP
(Makes 6 servings)

Remember when you were a kid how great a steaming bowl of tomato soup tasted with your favorite sandwich? There's a reason the classics never go out of style. Sometimes they just need to be updated. This tomato soup has all of the creamy texture you love and none of the fat you don't.

1	large onion, thinly sliced	1	bay leaf
1	tablespoon olive oil	½	teaspoon thyme
5	cups chicken broth	1	teaspoon parsley
½	cup chopped carrots	¾	teaspoon salt
½	cup peeled and chopped potatoes	½	teaspoon sugar
8	Roma tomatoes, peeled, seeded and cut into quarters	¼	teaspoon black pepper
		2	cups nonfat sour cream

In a large stockpot, sauté the onion in the olive oil over medium heat until translucent, about 5 minutes. Add the chicken broth, carrots, potatoes, tomatoes, bay leaf, thyme, and parsley and simmer for 20 to 25 minutes until the carrots and the potatoes are tender. Allow the soup to cool and process in batches until smooth. Stir in the salt, sugar, pepper, and sour cream. Serve immediately.

VEGETARIAN

CREAM OF CARROT SOUP
(Makes 6 servings)

Calories 163
Protein 6 g
Carbohydrate 29 g
Fat 3 g

Food group servings:
Vegetable 3
Milk/Yogurt 0.75
Fat 0.5

It's true. You can have creamy soup without a trace of cream. The secret of this velvety soup is a quick whirl in the blender and evaporated skim milk in place of heavy cream.

6 cups chicken or vegetable broth	1 (3-inch) piece fresh ginger root, peeled and grated
1 tablespoon olive oil	1 teaspoon ground nutmeg
2 pounds carrots, shredded	1 teaspoon salt
3 leeks, cleaned and sliced	1 teaspoon black pepper
1 sweet potato, peeled and diced	1 cup evaporated skim milk
4 stalks celery, chopped	

In a large stockpot, bring broth to a boil. Meanwhile, in a large nonstick skillet, heat the olive oil over medium heat and sauté carrots, leek, sweet potato, celery, ginger, and nutmeg for 10 to 15 minutes until soft. Add the sautéed vegetables to broth, reduce heat, and simmer for 30 minutes. Let the soup cool to room temperature and puree in batches in the blender until smooth. Return to the stockpot and cook over low heat until heated through. Season with salt and pepper; stir in the evaporated skim milk. Serve warm.

ASIAN WONTON SOUP

(Makes 4 servings)

Calories 389
Protein 31 g
Carbohydrate 51 g
Fat 8 g

Food group servings:
Grain 1
Vegetable 1
Protein 4
Fat 1.6

This soup is so easy and fast, it's sure to become a big favorite in your house.

2	quarts vegetable broth	1	(15-ounce) package frozen low-fat wontons
4	garlic cloves, thinly sliced		
1	(3-inch) piece ginger, peeled and thinly sliced	1	(15-ounce) can baby corn, drained and rinsed
8	ounces fresh shiitake mushrooms, stemmed, halved and thinly sliced	4	green onions, thinly sliced
		2	bunches watercress or arugula, stems removed

In a large stockpot combine the vegetable broth, garlic, and ginger and simmer gently for 10 minutes to infuse the flavors. Skim the garlic and ginger out of the broth and add the mushrooms, cooking until they begin to soften, about 10 minutes. Add the frozen wontons and the baby corn and boil until the wontons are tender, about 4 minutes. Stir in the green onions and watercress and cook until the watercress is wilted, about 30 minutes. Serve immediately.

TURKEY CHILI

(Makes 8 servings)

All you chili fans out there, gather 'round. This hearty chili has so much going for it in the flavor department that no one will even know it's low in fat. Feel free to add as much or as little spice as you like. (This recipe calls for beer, but you can substitute beef or chicken broth.)

Calories 335
Protein 45 g
Carbohydrate 20 g
Fat 8 g

Food group servings:
Grain 0.5
Vegetable 1
Protein 5
Fat 1.6

1	tablespoon olive oil	2	tablespoons Worcestershire sauce
2½	pounds ground turkey breast	1	to 3 tablespoons hot sauce
1	large onion, chopped	½	bottle light beer (the alcohol cooks out)
2	large bell peppers, chopped	1	(14-ounce) can tomato sauce
4	tablespoons chili powder	½	cup smoky barbecue sauce
2	tablespoons grill seasoning blend	2	cups corn kernels
1	tablespoon ground cumin		

Heat a large stockpot over medium-high heat. Add the olive oil, turkey, onions, and bell peppers and cook, breaking up the turkey, until the turkey is no longer pink and the vegetables are soft, 5 to 7 minutes. Add the chili powder, grill seasoning, cumin, Worcestershire sauce, and hot sauce. Add the beer and bring to a boil for a full minute to cook off the alcohol. Add the tomato sauce, barbecue sauce, and corn; simmer for 10 minutes and adjust seasonings as desired. Serve immediately.

Calories 175
Protein 12 g
Carbohydrate 29 g
Fat 2 g

Food group servings:
Grain 0.3
Vegetable 0.6
Protein 1.3
Fat 0.4

(VEGETARIAN)

VEGETARIAN CHILI
(Makes 7 servings)

You don't have to be a vegetarian to appreciate this chili. Carnivores will enjoy this hearty concoction, and not feel the least deprived.

1½ cups chopped onions

¾ cup chopped red bell pepper

¾ cup chopped green bell pepper

1 (14.5-ounce) can vegetable broth

2 (10-ounce) cans diced tomatoes with green chilies, undrained

½ cup salsa

1 tablespoon chili powder

1 teaspoon ground cumin

¾ teaspoon garlic powder

1 (15-ounce) can pinto beans, rinsed and drained

1 cup corn kernels

1 cup grated nonfat Cheddar cheese

In a slow cooker, combine the onions, bell peppers, vegetable broth, tomatoes, salsa, chili powder, cumin, garlic powder, pinto beans, and corn. Turn slow cooker on high. Cover and cook for 6 to 8 hours. Garnish with grated cheese.

Chapter 8

Vegetables and Side Dishes

No dinner is complete without a delicious vegetable! You can of course lightly steam fresh or frozen vegetables, but if your kids have resisted gobbling down their broccoli, peas, or carrots, here's a way to entice them—and to introduce them to some vegetables they may not have tried. In this chapter you'll also find delicious and healthier versions of some old favorites such as dinner rolls, mashed potatoes, and French fries.

QUICK 'N' EASY VEGETABLES

In a rush? No problem. Try one of these quick options to serve tasty vegetables you and your children need.

Quick vegetable 1:

▲ Steaming vegetables takes only a few minutes. Use an inexpensive steamer insert (it fits inside one of your pans), pour in a little water, and steam for a few minutes. One of the biggest mistakes people make with veggies is overcooking them—then they get soggy and lose their flavor, color, and crunch. Veggies are best when they still retain a bit of their snap. Keep a stock of frozen vegetables on hand: peas, broccoli, green beans, and whatever other veggies you like. (Of course fresh vegetables are wonderful, too.) Serve with lemon juice or garlic pepper sprinkled on top, or just a hint of liquid Butter Buds or Smart Balance Light.

Quick vegetable 2:

▲ Make a self-serve salad bar. Kids love making their own salads! Set out green leafy lettuces (not iceberg), carrots, corn, cooked beans, chopped turkey, shredded low-fat cheese, sunflower seeds, tomatoes, bell peppers, mushrooms, and low-fat dressing.

Quick vegetable 3:

▲ Cook small baked potatoes (one per family member) and allow each person to top a potato with a variety of choices: broccoli (steam in microwave), low-fat chili (from a can if you don't have any already made), shredded low-fat cheese, and other steamed or raw vegetables.

ROASTED ASPARAGUS WITH PARMESAN

(Makes 4 servings)

If you have trouble getting your kids to eat asparagus, try it roasted with a sprinkling of fresh Parmesan—they'll come around.

Calories 50
Protein 5 g
Carbohydrate 7 g
Fat 1 g

Food group servings:
Vegetable 2
Fat 0.2

2   bunches asparagus
     Nonfat olive oil cooking spray
     Salt and pepper, to taste

3   tablespoons grated Parmesan
     cheese

Preheat the oven to 400°.

Wash asparagus and pat dry with paper towels. Trim the woody ends and arrange the asparagus in a single layer in a roasting pan or jellyroll pan. Spray lightly with olive oil spray and sprinkle with salt and pepper. Roast for 10 minutes until crisp-tender. Sprinkle with Parmesan cheese and return to oven for 1 more minute to melt the cheese. Serve immediately.

SESAME ASPARAGUS

(Makes 6 servings)

If you haven't used dark sesame oil you don't know what you're missing. With just a drizzle, it transforms ordinary asparagus into something special. Make sure you look for dark sesame oil, not clear. The dark oil is made from toasted sesame seeds—the toasting brings out all the nutty sesame flavor of the seeds. You'll find it on the Chinese aisle of any major supermarket.

2	bunches asparagus	1	tablespoon dark sesame oil
½	cup water	2	teaspoons black sesame seeds

Cut the asparagus on an angle into 1-inch pieces and place in a large saucepan with the water. Lightly steam until crisp-tender, about 2 to 3 minutes. Drain and place in a serving dish. Toss the asparagus with the sesame oil and sprinkle with the seeds. Serve immediately.

AVOCADO-ORANGE SALAD

(Makes 4 servings)

This colorful and simple salad is sure to please. And if you do the slicing, your child can do the preparing.

For the salad:

2   navel oranges, peeled

1   large head Boston lettuce

2   small green onions, sliced

4   slices avocado

For the dressing:

1   tablespoon canola oil

1   teaspoon honey

2   tablespoons cider vinegar

Divide the oranges into sections, keeping 4 sections for the dressing. Cut the orange sections and tear the lettuce into bite-size pieces. Arrange the lettuce at the bottom of a bowl, and place the orange sections, onions, and avocado on top. For the dressing, blend the oil, honey, cider vinegar, and 4 remaining orange sections in a bowl. Pour the dressing over the salad, and toss lightly to mix.

Calories 80
Protein 2 g
Fat 6 g
Carbohydrate 7 g

Food group servings:
Vegetable 2
Fruit 0.5
Fat 1

Calories 96
Protein 5 g
Carbohydrate 11 g
Fat 5 g

Food group servings:
Vegetable 0.5
Protein 0.5
Fat 1

BROCCOLI SALAD

(Makes 4 servings)

This is a great way to get even your pickiest eater to eat broccoli. There are so many great flavors and textures going on in this salad: the crunch of the broccoli, the crisp bite of the carrots and water chestnuts, and the sweetness of the mandarin oranges—all perfectly complemented by the smoky turkey bacon. Your kids will never know it's good for them.

¼ cup low-fat mayonnaise	¼ cup sliced water chestnuts, drained
2 teaspoons sugar	
1 teaspoon cider vinegar	1 small can mandarin oranges, drained
2 cups fresh broccoli florets	
½ cup shredded carrots	2 tablespoons chopped red onion (optional)
¼ cup shredded low-fat Cheddar cheese	
	2 tablespoons cooked, crumbled turkey bacon

In a small bowl stir together the mayonnaise, sugar, and the vinegar. In a medium bowl combine the broccoli, carrots, Cheddar cheese, water chestnuts, mandarin oranges, and red onion. Pour the mayonnaise mixture over the vegetables and toss to coat. Sprinkle with the turkey bacon and cover and refrigerate for several hours to allow the flavors to develop.

ROASTED BRUSSELS SPROUTS

(Makes 6 servings)

Calories 49
Protein 4 g
Carbohydrate 10 g
Fat 0 g

Food group servings:
Vegetable 2

It's a safe bet that most of us have some bad childhood memories connected to this vegetable. But before you turn the page in disgust at the thought of serving Brussels sprouts, let me assure you these are not those mushy, over-boiled, grayish-green things you remember. They are completely different when they are roasted. They're sweet and crunchy and—yes, it's true—tasty.

1½ pounds Brussels sprouts	Salt and pepper, to taste
Nonfat olive oil spray	

Preheat the oven to 400°.

Wash the Brussels sprouts and pat dry on paper towels. Arrange in a single layer on a baking sheet. Spray lightly with olive oil spray and sprinkle with salt and pepper. Roast for 20 to 25 minutes until brown and crisp. Serve immediately.

ORANGE GINGER-GLAZED CARROTS

(Makes 6 servings)

Calories 69
Protein 1 g
Carbohydrate 17 g
Fat 0 g

Food group servings:
Vegetable 1.5

If ever there were a vegetable you could get kids to eat without argument, this is it. These carrots are sweet and vibrant and the ginger is the perfect complement.

1 (1-pound) package peeled baby carrots	¼ cup brown sugar
1 cup water	¼ cup orange juice
½ teaspoon ground ginger or 1 teaspoon grated fresh ginger root	2 tablespoons unseasoned rice vinegar
	Salt and pepper, to taste
	1 teaspoon Butter Buds granules

Combine the carrots and water in a shallow, microwave-safe bowl. Cover and microwave on high for 3 to 5 minutes until crisp-tender. Meanwhile, in a small saucepan, combine the ginger, brown sugar, orange juice, rice vinegar, salt and pepper, and Butter Buds granules. Bring to a boil over medium heat, reduce heat to a simmer, and cook for 10 minutes or until the liquid is reduced and syrupy. Drain the carrots and mix to coat them in the glaze. Serve immediately.

OVEN-ROASTED CARROTS

(Makes 6 servings)

Calories 65
Protein 2 g
Carbohydrate 15 g
Fat 0 g

Food group servings:
Vegetable 2.5

If your kids think they don't like carrots, chances are they haven't had them roasted. Roasting any vegetable at a high oven temperature really changes the flavor by slightly caramelizing the outside while the inside remains tender. The result is an intense, sweet flavor that's amazing.

2 pounds carrots, peeled and chunked	Nonfat olive oil spray Salt and pepper, to taste

Preheat the oven to 400°.

Place carrots in a roasting pan or jellyroll pan and lightly spray with olive oil spray and sprinkle with salt and pepper. Toss to coat and spread the carrots in a single layer. Roast in the oven for 30 to 40 minutes, stirring occasionally, until carrots are tender and caramelized around the edges. Serve immediately.

CAPRESE SALAD (BASIL AND MOZZARELLA)

(Makes 4 servings)

This colorful salad will make a big splash at your table all lined up in beautiful red, white, and green rows. Classic Caprese is drizzled with extra-virgin olive oil, but balsamic vinegar adds even more flavor and no fat, and gives a nice tang.

4	medium vine-ripened tomatoes		Salt and pepper, to taste
2	fresh mozzarella balls (packed in water)	¼	cup balsamic vinegar
12	fresh basil leaves		

Slice tomatoes and the mozzarella ¼ inch thick and arrange 3 slices of tomato and 2 slices of mozzarella alternately on 4 small plates, ending with tomato. Tuck 3 basil leaves between the tomatoes and cheese on each plate. Sprinkle with salt and pepper and drizzle with balsamic vinegar.

GARLIC GREEN BEANS

(Makes 3 servings)

Calories 118
Fat 0 g

Food group servings:
Vegetable 1.6

Simple—but tasty. No longer will your kids turn up their noses at green beans.

Nonfat cooking spray

1   tablespoon chopped garlic

2   cups cut green beans

Soy sauce, to taste

Black pepper, to taste

Spray a saucepan with nonfat cooking spray and sauté the chopped garlic. Add the green beans. Cook the beans, adding soy sauce and black pepper to taste. Stir and then cover the pan. When beans are crisp-tender, serve hot.

FIVE-A-DAY FOR GOOD HEALTH

You need a minimum of five servings a day of fruits and vegetables, and more can be better. These foods reduce the risk of cancer, heart disease, stroke, diabetes, and other diseases. They also have valuable nutrients and fiber, help fill you up, and can taste great!

The 5 A Day for Better Health national program, developed in 1991 as a partnership between the National Cancer Institute and the Produce for Better Health Foundation, promotes eating your fruits and veggies. (You can find lots of information at www.5aday.com and at www.cdc.gov/nccdphp/dnpa/5aday/.)

Serving sizes:

- 1 medium-size fruit
- ¾ cup (6 ounces) of 100% fruit or vegetable juice
- ½ cup fresh, frozen, or canned fruit (in 100% juice)
- ½ cup cooked vegetables
- 1 cup raw leafy greens
- 1 cup cooked vegetables
- ¼ cup dried fruit

Calories 64
Protein 3 g
Carbohydrate 8 g
Fat 3 g

Food group servings:
Vegetable 2
Fat 0.6

STEAM SAUTÉED GREEN BEANS

(Makes 6 servings)

The steam sauté method is one of my favorite ways to cook fresh vegetables for two reasons: It's incredibly easy and it lets the vegetables retain all their crunch and color. Try it with carrots, broccoli, cauliflower, or zucchini.

1	**pound fresh green beans, cleaned and trimmed**	⅓	**cup water**
	Zest of 1 lemon	¼	**cup chopped fresh Italian parsley**
2	**tablespoons liquid Butter Buds**	¼	**cup slivered almonds, toasted**

In a large saucepan over high heat, combine the green beans, lemon zest, Butter Buds, and water. Cover the saucepan with a tightly fitting lid until steam begins to escape around the edges of the lid, about 5 minutes. Remove the lid and sauté until the beans are crisp-tender, about 2 more minutes. Remove from heat and toss with chopped parsley and toasted almonds. Serve immediately.

GINGERY SUGAR SNAP PEAS

(Makes 6 servings)

Calories 24
Protein 1 g
Carbohydrate 11 g
Fat 0 g

Food group servings:
Vegetable 1

It's not easy to get kids interested in eating the green stuff on their plates, but if any vegetable can change that attitude, this is the one. Sugar snap peas are crisp, sweet, and delicious raw or cooked. The key is not to overcook them—they're at their best with some "snap" to them.

3 cups fresh sugar snap peas	1 teaspoon reduced-sodium soy sauce
½ cup water	
1 tablespoon liquid Butter Buds	1 pinch ground ginger
1 tablespoon orange or peach preserves	1 pinch black pepper

Remove the ends and the strings from the peas and lightly steam in a large saucepan with the water until crisp-tender, about 2 minutes. Drain well and set aside.

In the same saucepan combine the Butter Buds, preserves, soy sauce, ground ginger, and pepper. Heat gently to melt the preserves. Return the peas to the pan and stir to coat. Serve immediately.

Calories 53
Protein 1 g
Carbohydrate 12 g
Fat 0 g

Food group servings:
Vegetable 1.5

OVEN-ROASTED ORANGE BUTTERNUT SQUASH

(Makes 4 servings)

If you've never tried butternut squash, you don't know what you're missing. It's vibrant and orange and has a flavor somewhere between a sweet potato and pumpkin. The orange juice and the maple syrup in the recipe further enhance the sweetness of this delicious vegetable.

	Nonstick cooking spray	¼	teaspoon salt
1	pound peeled and seeded butternut squash, cut into ½-inch pieces	⅛	teaspoon black pepper
		1	pinch ground cinnamon
⅓	cup orange juice	1	tablespoon liquid Butter Buds
1	tablespoon reduced-calorie maple syrup		

Preheat the oven to 425°.

Lightly spray a baking sheet with nonstick cooking spray and place the squash on it. In a small bowl combine the orange juice, maple syrup, salt, pepper, cinnamon, and Butter Buds. Pour the mixture over the squash and toss to coat. Spread the squash in a single layer on the baking sheet and place in the oven for about 25 minutes, until the squash is tender. Serve immediately.

SPEEDY ACORN SQUASH

(Makes 4 servings)

Calories 70
Protein 1 g
Carbohydrate 11 g
Fat 3 g

Food group servings:
Vegetable 1
Fat 0.6

Sometimes the key to getting kids to eat their vegetables is variety. This squash will definitely "mix things up" at your dinner table.

2	small acorn squash	¼	cup chopped walnuts or pecans
1	cup applesauce	½	teaspoon ground cinnamon
1	tablespoon reduced-calorie maple syrup		

Wash and halve the squash, and remove the seeds. Place the squash halves, cut sides down, in a baking dish. Cover and cook in a microwave on high (100% power) for 6 to 9 minutes or until tender, changing their position halfway through if your microwave does not have a revolving base.

Meanwhile, combine the applesauce, maple syrup, nuts, and cinnamon. Spoon the applesauce mixture into the squash halves. Cook on high about 3 minutes more or until applesauce mixture is heated through.

TEMPT YOUR CHILDREN WITH FRUITS AND VEGGIES

Here are some nutrient-packed choices, and ways to serve them:

APPLES. Rich in soluble fiber, potassium, and vitamin C, one small apple contains only 80 calories. Apples can be enjoyed fresh, juiced, pureed, baked, and stewed. Slice a fresh apple into wedges and enjoy with a tablespoon of peanut butter for a filling snack. Tuck a cup of applesauce into your lunch sack for a healthful dessert. Bake a cored apple with a dash of cinnamon and brown sugar for a delicious winter treat.

BANANAS. The banana is a powerhouse of nutrients. One fruit provides more than 100% of your daily potassium needs, as well as 2 grams of protein and 4 grams of fiber. Raw and straight from the peel, frozen and blended with nonfat milk, mashed and served as a topping for cereals and fruit salads—any way you peel it, the banana's natural sweetness and creamy texture make it an indulgent treat. Store unripe bananas at room temperature—outside of the refrigerator—as they cannot ripen properly at cold temperatures. Once the bananas are ripe, you can refrigerate them for up to two weeks.

BROCCOLI. Broccoli is rich in vitamin A, folic acid, iron, magnesium, and zinc; a half-cup of cooked broccoli contains as much vitamin C as an orange, and as much calcium as a half-cup of milk. The sharp flavor of broccoli perfectly complements the creaminess of cheese and other dairy products, which makes this nutrient-rich vegetable very appealing to children. Try mixing cooked broccoli spears with a low-fat cheese sauce, or with nonfat sour cream atop a steaming baked potato.

CARROTS. Carrots are wonderful sources of vitamin A, which helps the body fight infection and keeps skin and hair healthy. The beta-carotene compound gives carrots their vivid orange color, which our bodies convert into vitamin A after we eat them. Carrots are naturally sweet and the raw vegetable is excellent for snacking—try munching on peeled baby carrots with hummus or a tablespoon of peanut butter. Carrots are also delicious when grated in salads or chopped and boiled in soups and stews.

GRAPES. Grapes are also packed with nutrients. Grapes are delicious eaten right off the vine. Try freezing bunches of grapes for a special summer treat. When selecting grapes in the supermarket, look for plump, brightly colored fruits that are tightly attached to their stems. Grapes do not ripen after being picked from the vine.

LETTUCE. Lettuce is rich in fiber, vitamin A, and potassium—and one serving contains only 9 calories! Experiment with different varieties of lettuce in fresh salads. Darker green lettuce leaves are more nutritious than lighter green leaves, so choose darker varieties such as romaine, watercress, red lettuce, and endive. Toss with colorful vegetables and fruit, such as carrots, bell pepper, tomato, cucumber, raisins, mandarin oranges, grapes, or pineapple. Adding fresh herbs such as parsley, chives, and basil adds additional flavor. And don't forget your favorite low-fat dressing!

ORANGES. Just one orange—or one cup of orange juice—contains 130% of your daily vitamin C requirement. Oranges are delicious raw—just peel the fruit and divide it into segments. Orange juice is a potent source of vitamin C, although the juice contains less fiber than the whole fruit. You can mix the juice with water or with other fruit juices and yogurt for a refreshing smoothie. Look for firm, heavy fruits with colorful, fine-textured skins.

TOMATOES. Tomatoes are a concentrated source of nutrients. Lycopene—a potent antioxidant compound—gives tomatoes their brilliant red color, and the jelly-like substance around the seeds contains a high concentration of vitamin C. Tomatoes are also rich in vitamin A and potassium. Tomatoes are delicious raw: slice them up for a brilliant addition to salads and sandwiches. Sweet yellow and red cherry tomatoes make a delicious snack. Cooked tomatoes are even more nutritious: Cooking frees the lycopene, making it easier for the body to digest. Try tomatoes in sauces and soups, or baked on pizza and in casseroles. When selecting tomatoes, choose firm, well-shaped, and fragrant fruits that are heavy for their size.

Bread and Potatoes

Kids love bread and potatoes—particularly their French fries—and there's no reason for them to do without. Try these singularly tasty versions of their favorites. The guaranteed result: happy kids, happy parents.

Calories 192
Protein 6 g
Carbohydrate 43 g
Fat 0 g

Food group servings:
Grain 2.9
Protein 0.5

CRISPY FRENCH FRIES
(Makes 4 servings)

They should be called "French Bakes," but somehow that doesn't have quite the same ring to it. These fries are so much better than anything you buy frozen, and so much more delicious—and they're fat free! What gives regular French fries that delicious crispy texture is fat, which conducts heat and seals the outside. Here, egg whites replace that coating and give the potatoes a crisp texture by sealing the French fry rather than steaming it, which would result in a soggier end product. (You can buy pasteurized egg whites for convenience instead of cracking eggs, if you prefer.) Experiment with your favorite seasonings: These are great with rosemary and garlic, or a little cayenne for kick.

	Nonstick cooking spray	1	teaspoon seasoned salt
2	extra-large egg whites	4	large Idaho potatoes

Preheat the oven to 400°.

Spray a baking sheet with nonstick cooking spray and set aside. In a large bowl combine the egg whites and the seasoned salt. Wash the potatoes and slice them lengthwise into ¼-inch ovals. Slice each oval into matchsticks and toss to coat in the egg white mixture. Place the potatoes in a single layer on the baking sheet, leaving a bit of space between. Bake for 35 to 45 minutes, turning with a spatula every 10 minutes to ensure even browning. Serve immediately.

SCALLOPED POTATOES

(Makes 8 servings)

When it comes to kids, you can never go wrong with potatoes. These potatoes, embellished with nonfat cheese and nonfat sour cream, will be the perfect side dish and the star of any meal.

Calories 184
Protein 14 g
Carbohydrate 39 g
Fat 0.2 g

Food group servings:
Grain 1.5
Protein 1
Fat 0.4

	Nonstick cooking spray	3	tablespoons nonfat milk
6	large potatoes	½	teaspoon salt
2	cups nonfat sour cream	¼	teaspoon black pepper
2	cups grated nonfat Cheddar cheese	⅓	cup seasoned Italian bread crumbs
¼	cup diced onions	2	tablespoons liquid Butter Buds

Preheat the oven to 350°.

Spray a 9 x 13-inch casserole dish with nonstick cooking spray and set aside. Pierce the potatoes in several places with a fork and microwave on high for 5 minutes, just until beginning to soften. Meanwhile, in a large bowl combine the sour cream, cheese, onions, milk, salt, and pepper. Set aside.

When the potatoes are cool enough to handle, peel and slice thin. Gently turn the potatoes in the sauce mixture and spoon into the casserole dish. Combine the bread crumbs with the Butter Buds and sprinkle over the top. Bake for 30 minutes until hot and bubbly and the bread crumbs are browned.

Calories 123
Protein 3 g
Carbohydrate 27 g
Fat 0 g

Food group servings:
Grain 1.8
Milk/Yogurt 0.2

MAGNIFICENT MASHED POTATOES

(Makes 8 servings)

You may already know how to make delicious mashed potatoes, but you may not know how to make them without all the fat and calories. Trust me, any fat that has been removed from this recipe has been replaced with lots of flavor.

16	ounces baby Dutch yellow potatoes, scrubbed	6	to 8 garlic cloves, minced
16	ounces baby red potatoes, scrubbed	½	to ⅔ cup evaporated skim milk
3	tablespoons liquid Butter Buds, divided	½	teaspoon salt
		½	teaspoon black pepper

Place the potatoes in a large stockpot with enough water to cover completely. Cover with a lid, bring to a boil, remove lid, and continue to boil until fork-tender.

Meanwhile, in a small nonstick skillet, heat 1 tablespoon of the Butter Buds and cook the garlic for about a minute. Reduce the heat and add the evaporated skim milk. Heat for 2 minutes just to warm through, but do not boil.

When the potatoes are done, drain well and return them to the pot. Beat with an electric mixer on low speed to break up the potatoes. Add the remaining Butter Buds, garlic, evaporated milk, salt, and pepper and continue to mash until fluffy.

MUSHROOM GRAVY

(Makes 6 servings)

Calories 89
Protein 6 g
Carbohydrate 14 g
Fat 1 g

Food group servings:
Milk/Yogurt 0.2
Fat 0.2

Everybody loves a good gravy over mashed potatoes, with chicken, or drizzled over turkey meat loaf. The problem is, it's laden with fat. This quick recipe isn't just delicious—it's also low in fat. Feel free to experiment and use vegetable, beef, or mushroom broth to really make it your own.

Nonstick cooking spray	¼ cup all-purpose flour
8 ounces sliced mushrooms	3 cups chicken broth
1 medium onion, diced	1 cup evaporated skim milk
1 garlic clove, minced	Salt and pepper, to taste
2 tablespoons liquid Butter Buds	

Spray a nonstick skillet with nonstick cooking spray and sauté the mushrooms, onion, and garlic over medium heat until the onions are soft, about 5 minutes. Remove and set aside. Add the liquid Butter Buds to the pan and bring to a bubble. Add the flour and cook for 1 minute to remove the raw taste. Increase the heat to medium-high and whisk in the chicken broth, stirring constantly to avoid lumps. Whisk in the evaporated skim milk and fold the mushroom mixture back in. Season with salt and pepper and allow the gravy to thicken and reduce to about 3 cups. Serve hot.

JALAPEÑO CORN BREAD

(Makes 10 servings)

Who can resist fresh hot corn bread right out of the oven? This bread is spiked with jalapeño for a little kick.

Nonstick cooking spray
¼ cup all-purpose flour
1 cup cornmeal
½ teaspoon salt
1½ teaspoons baking powder
½ cup egg substitute

½ (8-ounce) can cream-style corn
1 cup grated low-fat Cheddar cheese
½ cup low-fat buttermilk
½ cup liquid Butter Buds

Preheat the oven to 350°.

Spray a large cast-iron skillet with nonstick cooking spray and set aside. In a small bowl whisk together the flour, cornmeal, salt, and baking powder, and set aside. In a large bowl, beat the egg substitute until light and fluffy; mix in the corn, Cheddar cheese, buttermilk, and Butter Buds. Fold in the dry ingredients, mixing until well moistened. Pour the batter into the prepared skillet and bake for 50 to 60 minutes until a toothpick inserted in the middle comes out clean.

BAKED HUSH PUPPIES

(Makes 8 servings)

Calories 65
Protein 3 g
Carbohydrate 9 g
Fat 2 g

Food group servings:
Grain 0.5
Fat 0.4

Remember those delicious deep-fried hush puppies you'd get at your favorite fish 'n' chips joint? Of course they were so good, but so bad for you. We've come up with a way for you to enjoy that wonderful flavor and crunch with none of the fat. Because these little gems are baked, not fried, you can serve them without guilt.

	Nonstick cooking spray	⅛	teaspoon dried dill
¼	cup cornmeal	⅛	teaspoon cayenne pepper
¼	cup all-purpose flour	¼	cup egg substitute
¾	teaspoon baking powder	2	tablespoons nonfat milk
¼	teaspoon salt	2	tablespoons minced green onion
1	teaspoon sugar	1	tablespoon minced flat-leaf
¼	teaspoon garlic powder		parsley
¼	teaspoon celery seed		

Preheat the oven to 425°.

Spray a mini muffin pan with nonstick cooking spray and set aside. In a large bowl whisk together the cornmeal, flour, baking powder, salt, sugar, garlic powder, celery seed, dill, and cayenne pepper. Add the egg substitute and the milk to the dry ingredients and stir to combine. Gently fold in the green onion and the parsley. Spoon the batter by the rounded tablespoon into the muffin tin and bake for 15 to 20 minutes until golden brown. Serve immediately.

DELECTABLE DINNER ROLLS

(Makes 24 rolls)

Calories 124
Protein 4 g
Carbohydrate 25 g
Fat 1 g

Food group servings:
Grain 1.6
Fat 0.2

Forget those prepackaged refrigerator dinner rolls. Admittedly these take a bit longer, but the reward is a light, tender dinner roll reminiscent of the ones your favorite relative might have made at holiday time. This recipe makes two dozen rolls, but you can easily cut the recipe in half for a smaller crowd.

2	packages yeast	½	cup egg substitute
2	cups warm water	¼	cup liquid Butter Buds
½	cup sugar	5	cups all-purpose flour
1½	teaspoons salt		Nonstick cooking spray

In a large bowl dissolve the yeast in the warm water. Add the sugar, salt, egg substitute, Butter Buds, and 1 cup of the flour and beat with an electric mixer until smooth. Stir in the rest of the flour until well incorporated. Cover the dough with a clean towel and let rise in a warm place until it doubles in size, about 45 minutes.

Meanwhile, spray 2 muffin pans with nonstick cooking spray and preheat the oven to 400°.

Spoon the dough into the prepared muffin tins until the cups are about half full. Let the dough rise until it reaches the top of the muffin tins, about 20 to 30 minutes. Bake for 12 to 15 minutes until golden brown.

Dressings, Relish, and Salsa

Sometimes just what you need to enliven a plain dinner is a side dish of salsa or relish, or a zesty dressing for a tossed salad. Here's a great selection.

BUTTERMILK DRESSING
(Makes 8 servings, ¼ cup per serving)

This delicious dressing is a great substitute for ranch. Because it's made with buttermilk and nonfat sour cream, it's got that creamy texture you love with almost no fat. It's great on your favorite salad and as a dip for vegetables.

1 cup nonfat sour cream
1 cup low-fat buttermilk
2 tablespoons honey

2 green onions, minced
Salt and pepper, to taste

In a small bowl, whisk together the sour cream, buttermilk, and honey. Fold in the green onions and season with salt and pepper.

Calories 74
Protein 2 g
Carbohydrate 16 g
Fat 1 g

Food group servings:
Milk/Yogurt 0.1
Fat 0.2

THOUSAND ISLAND DRESSING
(Makes 4 servings, ¼ cup per serving)

This tastes just like your kids' favorite pink dressing, but is better for them. Try it as a dip for Crispy French Fries (see page 158).

1 cup nonfat mayonnaise
¼ cup chili sauce
3 hard-boiled egg whites, chopped
2 tablespoons finely chopped celery

2 tablespoons finely chopped onion
1 tablespoon sweet relish
½ teaspoon salt
½ teaspoon paprika

In a small bowl mix all ingredients together and stir to combine.

Calories 63
Protein 3 g
Carbohydrate 9 g
Fat 2 g

Food group servings:
Protein 0.4
Fat 0.4

HOW TO GET YOUR KIDS TO EAT VEGETABLES

When it comes to getting kids to eat their vegetables there's no doubt about it: this starts with you! If you haven't been regularly eating vegetables, don't be surprised if your kids turn up their noses when they suddenly find broccoli or asparagus on their plates.

But studies show that kids' food preferences are largely shaped by what's available to them, and persistence will pay off even when those "yucky green things" are initially rejected.

If you start your kids off early, you can end up with a preschooler who eagerly gobbles broccoli and green beans at lunchtime. Children's likes and dislikes don't change much from age three to eight, however, and new foods are most likely accepted at ages two to four than older.

So what do you do when your eight-year-old refuses to eat vegetables? Here are some ways to help turn your child into a veggie-lover.

SET AN EXAMPLE. Serve yourself salad and vegetables, and let your kids see you enjoying it. Comment on how tasty it is.

OFFER A CHOICE. If you let your children choose what vegetables they would like for their meal, they're more likely to eat them (suggest a few options, and make clear that French fries or mashed potatoes don't count).

INVOLVE THE CHILDREN. Have your kids help you choose and prepare the vegetable for the meal.

FLAVOR WITH DIP. Serve crunchy raw cut-up vegetables with low-fat ranch dip made with reduced-fat mayonnaise and a ranch seasoning packet.

BE CREATIVE. Maybe your child finds cooked spinach slimy but would enjoy it raw in a salad, or will chomp down broccoli if you serve it with dip.

WATCH IT GROW. Plant a small vegetable garden with your kids and let them tend it. Children are much more likely to try a vegetable they've nurtured themselves.

SERVE IN A DRINK. Some broccoli or spinach disguised with watermelon or apple juice won't taste like vegetables at all. Your kids won't even know they're in there.

TRY ONE BITE. Use a "one-bite" rule—everyone has to try at least one bite of a food each time it is served.

BE PERSISTENT. Kids don't always like things the first few times they are asked to try them, but keep serving new foods and keep eating them yourself.

ROAST VEGETABLES. Nobody likes soggy over-boiled Brussels sprouts or carrots, but roasting them at a high temperature results in a tender vegetable slightly caramelized on the outside that really brings out the natural sweetness. Broccoli, squash, asparagus, and bell peppers are all great candidates.

SERVE A SALAD BAR. Who doesn't like a great salad with lots of fresh toppings and a favorite dressing? Just make sure the dressing is low fat and remember, the darker the lettuce the more nutrients it has.

SNEAK IT IN. Grate zucchini into muffins or bread; grate carrots and slice celery into tuna salad; add chopped red pepper and onions to spaghetti sauce; put dark lettuce on sandwiches; slice plenty of veggies into a tasty stew.

TRY A STIR-FRY. Slice up carrots, onions, pepper, squash, mushrooms, or celery and stir-fry with a small amount of oil, along with beef or chicken sliced thin.

MAKE IT EASY. Have pre-bagged veggie snacks ready to go—sliced carrots, celery, bell pepper. For small children, serve bite-size pieces and pack in a plastic container in their lunches.

BE REALISTIC. Realize that a serving size for a toddler is as little as one tablespoon per year of age; for older children it is one whole fruit, half a cup of cooked vegetables, or one cup of raw vegetables.

BE PATIENT. Changes take time—but these are healthful lifetime habits you are helping your child build. Don't give up!

CAESAR SALAD DRESSING

(Makes 10 servings, ¼ cup per serving)

What kid doesn't love cool, creamy Caesar dressing? This light, easy-to-make version keeps well in the refrigerator, so keep it on hand for salads and as a dip.

½ cup egg substitute	½ teaspoon salt
4 tablespoons red wine vinegar	¼ teaspoon black pepper
2 garlic cloves, minced	¾ cup chicken broth
2 teaspoons Dijon mustard	½ cup liquid Butter Buds
2 teaspoons anchovy paste	¼ cup grated Parmesan cheese

In a blender combine the egg substitute, vinegar, garlic, Dijon mustard, anchovy paste, salt, and pepper. Cover and blend for several seconds until well combined. With the blender running, gradually add the chicken broth, Butter Buds, and Parmesan cheese. Serve well chilled.

GREEN GODDESS DRESSING

(Makes 8 servings, ¼ cup per serving)

This dressing is so retro it's cool again. It's great on everything from salad to vegetables. Don't let the anchovy paste scare you. It lends a salty, slightly nutty quality to the dressing and your kids will never know it's there.

1 clove garlic, minced	½ cup nonfat sour cream
1 tablespoon anchovy paste	⅓ cup chopped parsley
4 tablespoons chopped chives	3 tablespoons nonfat milk
2 tablespoons lemon juice	¼ teaspoon black pepper
2 tablespoons white wine vinegar	
1 cup nonfat mayonnaise	

Combine all ingredients in a blender and blend until smooth.

POPPY SEED DRESSING

(Makes 10 servings, ¼ cup per serving)

This dressing is the perfect combination of sweet and tart. Try it on your favorite salad or fresh fruit.

⅓ cup grated white onion

1½ cups Splenda Granular

2 teaspoons dry mustard

1 teaspoon salt

⅔ cup white vinegar

2 cups liquid Butter Buds

2 tablespoons poppy seeds

Place all ingredients in the blender and blend until smooth.

Calories 77
Protein 0 g
Carbohydrate 19 g
Fat 0 g

Food group servings:
None

MANGO BLACK BEAN SALSA

(Makes 5 servings)

This recipe is so "California Cuisine," but not at all fussy and pretentious. It's cool and refreshing and a great pairing with chicken or fish (try with our Sweet-Spicy Glazed Salmon on page 98).

1 (16-ounce) package frozen mango chunks, thawed

½ red bell pepper, diced

½ jalapeño pepper, deseeded, minced

½ hothouse cucumber, chopped

½ (14-ounce) can black beans, drained and rinsed

Juice of 1 lime

Salt and pepper, to taste

3 tablespoons chopped cilantro

Chop the mango chunks a bit smaller than they come in the package. In a medium bowl combine the mango, red bell pepper, jalapeño, cucumber, black beans, lime juice, and salt and pepper. Stir in the chopped cilantro and allow the flavors to develop for 30 minutes at room temperature.

Calories 65
Protein 1 g
Carbohydrate 17 g
Fat 0 g

Food group servings:
Fruit 1

TOMATO SALSA

(Makes 5 servings)

Calories 53
Protein 2 g
Carbohydrate 12 g
Fat 1 g

Food group servings:
Vegetable 1.6
Fat 0.2

I bet you didn't know how easy it is to make your own salsa from scratch. In almost the time it takes you to open that jar of so-called salsa sitting in your pantry, you can make it fresh. Almost. Serve this with baked tortilla chips and vegetables.

8	Roma tomatoes, seeded and diced	1	teaspoon salt
			Juice of 1 lime
1	jalapeño, chopped	½	cup diced red onion
2	cloves garlic, minced	2	tablespoons chopped cilantro

Place 3 tomatoes, jalapeño, garlic, salt, and lime juice in a blender and pulse just until blended. Transfer to a small bowl and stir in the remaining tomatoes, diced red onion, and chopped cilantro. Stir to combine and let the flavors develop for 30 minutes at room temperature.

CRANBERRY ORANGE RELISH

(Makes 4 servings)

Calories 98
Protein 1 g
Carbohydrate 25 g
Fat 0 g

Food group servings:
Fruit 1

This fresh relish might be a little different than that congealed jelly from a can you're used to serving at holiday time. But trust me, it's so much better and the flavor is so much brighter than that congealed stuff, and it's not much more work than opening a can.

2	cups fresh cranberries, washed	¼	cup sugar
1	whole orange, cut into wedges		

Place cranberries, orange pieces (skin and all), and sugar in the bowl of a food processor fitted with a blade attachment. Pulse several times until coarsely chopped. Let stand at room temperature for 30 minutes to allow the flavors to develop.

Chapter 9

Desserts

No one ever said that eating healthily meant that you had to forego dessert—at least we didn't! Most desserts are filled with sugar and fat (or else are tasteless), but not our delicious versions.

QUICK 'N' EASY DESSERTS

No time to cook? Never fear. You can toss together a quick dessert in minutes.

Quick dessert 1:

▲ Instant pudding made with sugar-free pudding mix and nonfat milk

Quick dessert 2:

▲ 3 graham cracker squares spread with frozen nonfat yogurt, topped with sliced strawberries

Quick dessert 3:

▲ Trail Mix: 1 tablespoon unsweetened cereal, 1 to 2 tablespoons dried fruit (raisins, dried apricots, dried apples), 2 tablespoons nuts or seeds, 1 teaspoon coconut, 1 teaspoon chocolate chips (makes 1 serving)

Kids' Classic

CHOCOLATE CHIP COOKIES

(Makes 24 cookies; 24 servings, 1 cookie per serving)

Calories 85
Protein 1 g
Carbohydrate 7 g
Fat 6 g

Food group servings:
Grain 0.5
Fat 1

These cookies make a great after-school snack for hungry kids on the go.

	Butter-flavored nonstick cooking spray	1	tablespoon vanilla extract
		1	cup all-purpose flour
½	cup butter or margarine	½	teaspoon baking soda
⅓	cup Splenda Sugar Blend for Baking	¼	teaspoon salt
		½	cup mini chocolate chips
¼	cup egg substitute	½	cup chopped pecans

Preheat the oven to 375°.

Spray two baking sheets with nonstick cooking spray and set aside. In a large bowl beat the margarine and Splenda with an electric mixer until fluffy. Mix in the egg substitute and vanilla extract. In a small bowl whisk together the flour, baking soda, and salt, then mix the dry ingredients into the wet. Gently fold in the mini chocolate chips and the chopped pecans. Drop the dough by the rounded tablespoon onto the prepared baking sheet and flatten with the bottom of a drinking glass sprayed with nonstick cooking spray. Bake for 8 to 10 minutes and cool on a wire rack.

ABOUT SUGAR SUBSTITUTES

You're right to be concerned about the use of artificial sweeteners, because of possible health risks and because you don't want to encourage your child to crave sweet foods.

But because of the health risks of a child being overweight, and because it can be really difficult for a child not to have cookies and brownies like other kids, we have included some dessert recipes that use sugar combined with a sugar substitute. (Recipes such as cakes, breads, brownies, and cookies depend on sugar for browning and volume, and would not turn out well using a sugar substitute alone.)

If you prefer not to use sugar substitute, avoid these recipes or try them with an equivalent amount of sugar. (You'd actually need to double the amount of Splenda Sugar Blend for Baking for the same amount of sweetness, but you might want to try the recipe with a lesser amount of sugar—think of it as an experiment!) To help keep track of calories: One cup of sugar has 770 calories and 192 grams of carbohydrates; one teaspoon of sugar has 16 calories and 4 grams of carbohydrates.

Here are some details about sugar substitutes:

EQUAL. Made from aspartame, this sweetener may lose sweetness while baking, so makers recommend Equal Sugar Lite for baking. You could, however, use regular Equal in dishes such as fruit pies, drinks, and sauces. Calories: Regular Equal and Equal Spoonful have no calories; Equal Sugar Lite has half the calories and carbohydrates of sugar. Meaurements: 1 packet Equal = 2 teaspoons sugar; 1 cup Equal Spoonful or Equal Sugar Lite = 1 cup sugar.

SPLENDA. Made from sucralose, this can be used in baking. For recipes where volume, moisture, and texture are important, such as cakes, brownies, and muffins, Splenda Sugar Blend for Baking would work best. Calories: Regular Splenda and Splenda Granular have none; Splenda Sugar Blend for Baking has half the calories and carbs as sugar. Measurements: 1 packet Splenda = 2 teaspoons sugar; 1 cup Splenda Granular = 1 cup sugar; ½ cup Splenda Sugar Blend for Baking = 1 cup sugar.

SWEET'N LOW. Made from saccharin, this can be used in recipes for sauces and drinks. For baked goods, however, you would substitute half the sugar in a recipe with the equivalent amount of Sweet'N low. Calories: None. Measurements: 1 packet Sweet'N Low = 2 teaspoons sugar; 8 teaspoons Sweet'N Low (or 2 teaspoons Sweet'N Low liquid) = 1 cup sugar.

Once your child has reached his or her ideal weight, you may consider switching to honey or sugar in recipes. You can serve smaller portions of desserts—served with sliced fruit or nonfat whipped topping so your child doesn't feel short-changed.

Kids' Classic

OATMEAL RAISIN COOKIES

(Makes 48 cookies; 24 servings, 2 cookies per serving)

Calories 144
Protein 3 g
Carbohydrate 27 g
Fat 3 g

Food group servings:
Grain 1
Fruit 0.2
Fat 0.6

Whenever you take the fat out of a recipe, it's important to replace what you've taken away with flavor. The addition of allspice and cinnamon really add a nice "something" to this cookie, and the yogurt and the milk help keep it moist. Like all baked goods, it's important not to overbake.

	Nonstick cooking spray	½	teaspoon salt
½	cup oat bran	3	cups rolled oats
½	cup whole wheat-flour	1¼	cups raisins
½	cup all-purpose flour	¼	cup canola oil
¼	teaspoon allspice	2	tablespoons nonfat yogurt
½	teaspoon ground cinnamon	½	cup nonfat milk
1	teaspoon baking soda	3	egg whites
1	teaspoon Butter Buds granules	2	teaspoons vanilla
1	cup lightly packed brown sugar		

Preheat the oven to 375°. Cover a baking sheet with parchment or waxed paper or aluminum foil. Spray the foil with nonstick cooking spray.

In a small bowl, whisk together the oat bran, flours, allspice, cinnamon, baking soda, Butter Buds, brown sugar, and salt. Stir in the oats and raisins. In another large bowl, combine the canola oil, yogurt, milk, egg whites, and vanilla. Mix the dry ingredients into the wet and stir until well combined. Drop the dough by the tablespoon onto the prepared baking sheet and bake for 15 minutes, or until golden. Remove the cookies to a wire rack to cool.

Calories 115
Protein 1 g
Carbohydrate 18 g
Fat 4 g

Food group servings:
Grain 0.85
Fat 0.2

LEMON BARS

(Makes 9 bars; 9 servings)

Cool and lemony, these bars are one of my favorite reasons to bake.

For the crust:

Nonstick cooking spray

¾ cup all-purpose flour

3 tablespoons sugar

¼ cup butter or margarine, cut into small pieces

For the filling:

¼ cup egg substitute

1 egg white

⅔ cup sugar

2 tablespoons all-purpose flour

1 teaspoon lemon zest

2 tablespoons lemon juice

1 tablespoon water

¼ teaspoon baking powder

Powdered sugar (optional, for dusting the top)

Preheat the oven to 350°.

Lightly coat an 8-inch square baking pan with nonstick cooking spray and set aside.

To make the crust, whisk together the flour and the 3 tablespoons sugar in a small bowl. Using a pastry blender, cut in the butter or margarine until the mixture is crumbly and resembles coarse meal. Press the mixture into the bottom of the prepared pan and bake for 15 minutes until golden brown on the edges.

Meanwhile, for the filling, in a small bowl combine the egg substitute and egg white and beat with an electric mixer on medium speed until frothy. Add the ⅔ cup sugar, flour, lemon zest, lemon juice, water, and baking powder and beat on medium speed for about 3 minutes until the mixture thickens slightly. Pour the filling over the hot crust.

Bake for 20 to 25 minutes or until the edges are brown and the center is set. Allow to cool completely and cut into 9 squares. Cut each square diagonally to make a triangle. Sift powdered sugar lightly over the tops of the lemon bars.

Kids' Classic

BROWNIES

(Makes 12 brownies; 12 servings)

Calories 94
Protein 2 g
Carbohydrate 13 g
Fat 5 g

Food group servings:
Grain 0.3
Milk/Yogurt 0.3
Fat 1

These will be the hit of your child's next bake sale—and of course you'll be the hero among parents when you let slip that these gooey brownies only have 5 grams of fat each.

Nonstick cooking spray
2 ounces unsweetened baking chocolate
½ cup nonfat vanilla yogurt
½ cup all-purpose flour
3 tablespoons unsweetened cocoa powder
½ teaspoon baking soda
¼ teaspoon salt
⅙ cup Splenda Sugar Blend for Baking
½ cup chopped pecans

Preheat the oven to 350°.

Spray an 8-inch baking pan with nonstick cooking spray and set aside. Melt the chocolate in a microwave-safe bowl on medium power for 1 minute. Set aside to cool. In another medium bowl, combine the yogurt, flour, cocoa, baking soda, salt, and Splenda. Stir in the cooled melted chocolate and pecans. Pour into prepared pan and bake for 20 to 22 minutes.

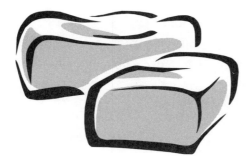

Calories 116
Protein 2 g
Carbohydrate 24 g
Fat 1 g

Food group servings:
Grain 0.3
Fruit 0.5
Fat 0.5

BROWNIE FRUIT PIZZA

(Makes 12 servings)

Every kid loves pizza for dinner, pizza for breakfast, but how about pizza for dessert? This is a fun and easy way to get your kids to eat more fruit.

For the crust:
Nonstick cooking spray
3   tablespoons butter or margarine, room temperature
¼   cup Splenda Sugar Blend for Baking
¼   cup egg substitute
⅔   cup all-purpose flour
¾   cup chocolate syrup, plus more for drizzling

Toppings:
3   cups assorted fresh fruit, such as strawberries, kiwifruit, peaches, bananas, mandarin oranges, raspberries, and blueberries

Preheat the oven to 350°.

Lightly coat a 12-inch pizza pan with nonstick cooking spray and set aside.

In a medium mixing bowl beat the butter and Splenda until smooth. Slowly add the egg substitute and beat well. Alternately add the flour and chocolate syrup, beating on low speed after each addition until well combined. Spread the mixture over the prepared pizza pan.

Bake for about 20 minutes or until the top springs back when lightly touched. Allow the crust to cool completely on a wire rack.

To serve, arrange the fruit on top of the brownie crust and slice into 12 equal wedges. Drizzle each wedge with a bit of chocolate syrup.

FRUIT PIZZA

(Makes 12 servings)

This recipe is fast, easy for your kids to make—and delicious. The perfect after-school snack.

24 graham cracker squares
8   ounces nonfat nondairy whipped topping, thawed
1   cup sliced strawberries
1   cup peeled and sliced peaches
1   cup sliced bananas
1   cup blueberries
½   cup all-fruit strawberry jam

Set graham cracker squares on a serving plate. Spread each piece with about 2 tablespoons of the nondairy whipped topping. Layer with pieces of each type of fruit. Top each cracker with 1 tablespoon of the all-fruit strawberry jam. Serve immediately or refrigerate until ready to serve.

Calories 123
Protein 1 g
Carbohydrates 27 g
Fat 2 g

Food group servings:
Grain 1
Fruit 1

YUMMY CHEESECAKE WITH BROWNIE CRUST

(Makes 12 servings)

Calories 91
Protein 10.7 g
Carbohydrate 16 g
Fat 1 g

Food group servings:
Grain 0.5
Protein 1
Fat 2.2

This cheesecake is so good you'll never believe how healthy it is.

For the crust:

¾ cup all-purpose flour

⅓ cup Splenda Sugar Blend for Baking

¼ cup unsweetened cocoa

½ teaspoon baking powder

¼ teaspoon salt

¼ cup applesauce

2 teaspoons chocolate extract

2 egg whites

Nonstick cooking spray

For the filling:

3 (8-ounce) packages nonfat cream cheese

1 cup Splenda Granular

2 teaspoons vanilla extract

¼ cup egg substitute

2 egg whites

Preheat the oven to 350°.

Spray a springform pan with nonstick cooking spray and set aside. In a medium bowl combine the flour, ⅓ cup Splenda Sugar Blend, cocoa, baking powder, and salt. Stir in the applesauce, chocolate extract, and egg whites until well combined. Pour the brownie mixture into the prepared springform pan and bake for 10 minutes. Remove the brownie crust from the oven and allow to cool slightly.

Reduce the oven temperature to 325°.

Meanwhile, in another medium bowl beat together the cream cheese and 1 cup Splenda Granular until fluffy. Add the vanilla, egg substitute, and egg whites, beating well to combine. Pour the cheesecake mixture over the brownie crust and smooth the top. Bake for 45 to 55 minutes (check it at 45 minutes; cooking time will vary) until almost set in the middle. Cool completely and serve well chilled.

STRAWBERRY CAKE

(Makes 12 servings)

Calories 138
Protein 2.5 g
Carbohydrate 30 g
Fat 1.3 g

Food group servings:
Grain 1
Fruit 1

4   tablespoons sugar

¼   cup warm water

2   to 3 quarts strawberries,
     washed and sliced

1   prebaked bundt-style angel food
     cake
     Nonfat nondairy whipped top-
     ping (optional)

Add sugar and water to the sliced strawberries and mix. Refrigerate for 3 hours or until a syrup has been made. Meanwhile, make 3 horizontal slices through the angel food cake, creating 3 layers. Place the bottom layer into a bundt pan and spoon strawberries and syrup onto the cake. Add the second layer of cake and repeat; then add the third layer of cake. Set aside the remaining strawberries. Place a heavy pan on top of the cake and refrigerate for 1 hour. Serve the cake by topping with more strawberries and nonfat whipped topping.

Calories 207
Protein 4 g
Carbohydrate 48 g
Fat 2.5 g

Food group servings:
Grain 0.7
Fat 0.5
Protein 0.25

CHOCOLATY CHOCOLATE CAKE

(Makes 12 servings)

Who says you can't have your cake and eat it too? This cake is so moist and chocolaty, your kids won't be able to resist. For that matter, neither will you. You can serve it as is, or with our Chocolate Sauce (page 190).

	Nonstick cooking spray	¼	teaspoon salt
¾	cup Splenda Sugar Blend for Baking	½	cup nonfat mayonnaise
1¼	cups all-purpose flour	½	teaspoon vinegar
½	cup unsweetened cocoa powder	½	cup prune juice
½	teaspoon baking soda	½	cup water
		1	teaspoon vanilla

Preheat the oven to 350°.

Spray an 8-inch square baking pan with nonstick spray and set aside. In a large bowl whisk together the Splenda, flour, cocoa powder, baking soda, and salt. With an electric mixer blend in the mayonnaise, vinegar, prune juice, water, and vanilla until smooth. Pour the batter into the prepared pan and bake for 40 to 50 minutes or until the cake springs back in the center when touched lightly.

Remove cake from the oven and allow to cool for 10 minutes. Using a wooden skewer, poke several holes in the cake about 2 inches apart and pour the chocolate sauce over the cake. Allow cake to cool completely before serving.

CHOCOLATE ORANGE CAKE

(Makes 10 servings)

Remember those chocolate oranges you used to get around the holidays that you would whack against the counter to break into sections? This is that flavor in cake form. What else do I need to say?

Nonstick cooking spray
¼ cup egg substitute
¾ cup Splenda Sugar Blend for Baking
½ cup low-fat buttermilk
2 teaspoons applesauce
2 tablespoons orange juice

1 teaspoon orange zest
1 teaspoon vanilla
1 cup self-rising flour
1 teaspoon baking soda
½ cup mini semisweet chocolate morsels
Cocoa powder, for garnish

Preheat the oven to 350°.

Spray a bundt pan with nonstick cooking spray and set aside. In a medium bowl beat the egg substitute and Splenda with an electric mixer until pale yellow and thick. Mix in the buttermilk, applesauce, orange juice, orange zest, vanilla, flour, and baking soda. Gently fold in the mini chocolate morsels and pour the batter into the prepared bundt pan. Bake for 25 to 30 minutes until a toothpick inserted in the middle comes out clean. Cool completely and turn out onto a plate. Dust with cocoa powder before serving.

Calories 189
Protein 3 g
Carbohydrate 35 g
Fat 4 g

Food group servings:
Grain 0.6
Protein 0.4
Fat 0.8

STRAWBERRY SHORTCAKE

(Makes 8 servings)

Calories 219
Protein 5 g
Carbohydrate 32 g
Fat 8 g

Food group servings:
Grain 1
Fruit 0.75
Fat 1.6

This is an updated version of a summer classic—with less than half the fat and calories. What could be better?

For the topping:

1   tablespoon sugar

3   cups sliced fresh strawberries

For the shortcakes:

1²⁄₃ cups all-purpose flour

1   tablespoon sugar

2   teaspoons baking powder

¼   teaspoon baking soda

3   tablespoons butter or margarine, cut into small pieces

¼   cup egg substitute

½   cup low-fat buttermilk

2   cups frozen light whipped dessert topping or 1 (1.3-ounce) envelope whipped dessert topping mix

In a medium bowl sprinkle 1 tablespoon of sugar over the berries. Stir to combine and set aside at room temperature for at least an hour to let the fruit produce juice.

Preheat the oven to 450°.

In another medium bowl whisk together the flour, sugar, baking powder, and baking soda. With a pastry blender, cut in the margarine until the mixture is crumbly and resembles coarse meal. Combine the egg substitute and the buttermilk. Make a well in the center of the flour mixture. Pour in the liquid all at once. Using a fork, stir from the outside toward the center just until moistened. Drop the dough in eight equal portions onto an ungreased cookie sheet.

Bake for 7 to 8 minutes until golden brown. Cool the shortcakes on a wire rack for about 10 minutes. Meanwhile, if using dessert topping mix, prepare according to package directions using nonfat milk.

To serve, cut the shortcakes into halves horizontally. Place the bottom half on a plate and top with strawberries and whipped topping. Top with the remaining half of the shortcake.

INDIVIDUAL APPLE CRUMBLE
(Makes 4 servings)

Kids love anything in individual-size portions and this apple crumble is no exception. Although it won't take a gimmick to get most kids to eat this dessert. It's wonderful. (You can of course make it in one large dish if you prefer.)

For the filling:

4   Granny Smith apples, peeled and thinly sliced

Juice of 1 lemon

For the topping:

¼   cup all-purpose flour

¼   cup oatmeal

⅓   cup brown sugar

½   teaspoon ground cinnamon

¼   teaspoon nutmeg

2½ tablespoons liquid Butter Buds

Preheat the oven to 350°.

Peel and slice the apples and toss with the lemon juice. Layer them into 4 ramekins (small baking dishes) and set aside. Meanwhile, in a small bowl combine the flour, oatmeal, brown sugar, cinnamon, nutmeg, and Butter Buds; stir with a fork to combine. Sprinkle the topping over the apples and bake for 35 to 40 minutes until the top is golden brown and the apples are tender. Serve warm.

Calories 200
Protein 2 g
Carbohydrate 49 g
Fat 1 g

Food group servings:
Grain 0.5
Fruit 1.6
Fat 0.2

Calories 227
Protein 2 g
Carbohydrate 39 g
Fat 9 g

Food group servings:
Grain 1
Fruit 2
Fat 1.8

APPLE BROWN BETTY

(Makes 6 servings)

I've never come across an apple dessert I didn't like, even if many of them do have almost "too cutesy" titles. This is certainly no exception and I know that your little ones will love it too.

1½ cups day-old whole-wheat bread crumbs (not packaged)

¼ cup butter or margarine, melted

3 cups peeled and sliced Granny Smith apples

½ cup light brown sugar

1½ teaspoons ground cinnamon

½ teaspoon allspice

¼ teaspoon nutmeg

¾ teaspoon salt

1 teaspoon grated lemon zest

2 tablespoons lemon juice

2 teaspoons vanilla

1 cup raisins

6 tablespoons apple juice concentrate, thawed

Preheat the oven to 350°.

In a small bowl combine bread crumbs and butter or margarine and press half of the mixture in the bottom of a 9-inch pie dish. In another bowl, combine apples, brown sugar, cinnamon, allspice, nutmeg, salt, lemon zest, lemon juice, vanilla, raisins, and apple juice concentrate. Pour the apple filling into the pie dish and top with remaining bread crumbs. Cover and bake for 35 minutes. Increase oven temperature to 400°. Uncover and bake for 20 minutes more. Serve warm with frozen nonfat vanilla yogurt.

BAKED APPLES À LA MODE

(Makes 5 servings)

This is quite possibly dessert nirvana. Enough said.

Calories 185
Protein 2.4 g
Carbohydrate 44 g
Fat 1.6 g

Food group servings:
Milk/Yogurt 0.2
Fruit 0.8
Fat 0.3

2   Granny Smith apples
¼   cup raisins
2   tablespoons red cinnamon
     candies
1   tablespoon packed brown sugar
⅓   cup apple juice
⅓   cup caramel sauce
1   tablespoon reduced-calorie
     maple syrup
1   cup vanilla low-fat frozen yogurt
     Chopped toasted walnuts, for
     garnish

Preheat the oven to 350°.

Core the apples and peel a strip from the top of each. Place the apples in a 2-quart square baking dish. In a medium bowl, combine the raisins, cinnamon candies, and brown sugar. Spoon the mixture into the center of each apple. Pour the apple juice into the baking dish. Bake, uncovered, for 50 to 55 minutes until the apples are tender, basting occasionally during baking.

Meanwhile, in a small bowl combine the caramel sauce and maple syrup and set aside. To serve, cut the apples in half lengthwise and place in dessert dishes with a scoop of vanilla yogurt. Drizzle with topping and sprinkle with walnuts.

SO-GOOD-YOU-WON'T-BELIEVE-IT CHOCOLATE PUDDING

(Makes 6 servings)

Chocolate pudding, anyone? Forget those little boxes of cook-and-serve pudding powder. This is so much better! I'm talking "lick your bowl clean, can't wait for dessert" better. Sure, it takes a little more time to make pudding from scratch. But store-bought pudding is filled with mystery ingredients and fillers and preservatives and sodium. It's much better to involve your kids, teaching them to enjoy cooking and to know exactly what they're eating.

⅓	cup sugar	2¼	cups nonfat milk
3	tablespoons all-purpose flour	2	teaspoons butter or margarine
3	tablespoons unsweetened cocoa powder	1½	teaspoons vanilla extract

In a heavy-bottomed medium saucepan stir together the sugar, flour, and cocoa powder. Add about ¼ cup of the milk and stir until dry ingredients are moistened, then add the remaining milk and mix well. Cook, stirring, over medium heat until the mixture just starts to come to a boil. Reduce heat to low and cook for 1 minute more. Remove from heat and stir in the butter and vanilla.

Spoon the pudding into 6 dessert cups and cover with plastic wrap. Make sure the plastic is touching the surface of the pudding to prevent a skin from forming. Chill for at least 4 hours before serving.

VANILLA PUDDING

(Makes 4 servings)

For those times when it just has to be vanilla.

Calories 211
Protein 11 g
Carbohydrate 37 g
Fat 2 g

Food group servings:
Milk/Yogurt 0.5
Protein 1
Fat 0.4

4	egg whites	½	cup sugar
1½	cups nonfat milk	¼	cup egg substitute
½	cup evaporated skim milk	1½	teaspoons vanilla extract
2	tablespoons cornstarch		

In a medium bowl whip the egg whites until soft but not dry peaks form. Meanwhile, in a large saucepan over medium heat combine the milk, evaporated milk, and cornstarch, and stir to dissolve. Add the sugar, egg substitute, and beaten egg whites and stir until the mixture comes to a boil. Reduce the heat to low and cook, whisking constantly, until the mixture becomes thick and creamy, about 5 minutes. Remove from heat and stir in the vanilla. Cool the pudding, spoon into 4 dessert cups, and cover with plastic wrap. Make sure the plastic is touching the surface of the pudding to prevent a skin from forming. Chill for at least 4 hours before serving.

CHOCOLATE SAUCE

(Makes 8 servings)

Ooey, gooey, chocolaty and warm. Need I say more? It's great with our Chocolaty Chocolate Cake (page 182) or drizzled atop nonfat frozen yogurt.

¾ cup Splenda Sugar Blend for Baking	1 cup Dutch processed unsweetened cocoa
1 cup water	1 tablespoon vanilla

In a medium saucepan, combine the Splenda and water and bring to a boil. Cook for 5 minutes. Remove from heat and whisk in the cocoa, stirring constantly. Return to low heat and continue to cook for 5 minutes. Remove from heat again and stir in the vanilla. Serve warm.

ICE CREAMY PARFAIT

(Makes 4 servings)

This fruity concoction is a favorite in the KidShape program.

2 large bananas, sliced	2 cups vanilla low-fat frozen yogurt
2 cups fresh or chilled raspberries	¼ cup low-fat granola

On bottom of each glass or cup, put one-fourth of the banana slices. Then add half the raspberries and ½ cup of frozen yogurt. For the last layer, add the rest of the bananas and top off with granola.

CHAPTER 10

Meal Plans

You've looked at all our great recipes, but getting started may seem daunting. Here's a great way to kick off your new lifestyle. We've set up three weeks of menu plans for you, using the recipes in this book and some foods you'll find in your grocery store. We have offered four calorie levels—1,200; 1,500; 1,800; and 2,200 calories. Your doctor may have suggested a daily calorie intake for your child, and the "Calorie Needs" chart on page 13 explains simple guidelines.

If you have different family members who need varying calorie levels, this can be tricky, as you don't want one child to feel singled out. In this case, you'll want to adjust the menu plans so the meals you share as a family offer the same foods to everyone, in portion sizes that suit the child's energy needs.

Day 1	1,200 Calories — Foods	Food group servings	1,500 Calories — Foods	Food group servings	1,800 Calories — Foods	Food group servings	2,200 Calories — Foods	Food group servings
Breakfast	¾ cup bran cereal	1 Grain	¾ cup bran cereal	1 Grain	¾ cup bran cereal	1 Grain	¾ cup bran cereal	1 Grain
	8 ounces nonfat milk	1 Milk	8 ounces nonfat milk	1 Milk	8 ounces nonfat milk	1 Milk	8 ounces nonfat milk	1 Milk
Snack	1 small banana	1 Fruit	1 small banana	1 Fruit	1 small banana	1 Fruit	1 small banana	1 Fruit
					½ bagel with 1 tsp low-fat cream cheese	1 Grain 0.3 Fat	½ bagel with 1 tsp low-fat cream cheese	1 Grain 0.3 Fat
Lunch	Tuna Salad (page 40)	1.8 Protein 0.2 Fat	Tuna Salad (page 40)	1.8 Protein 0.2 Fat	Tuna Salad (page 40)	1.8 Protein 0.2 Fat	Tuna Salad (page 40)	1.8 Protein 0.2 Fat
	1 slice whole-wheat bread	1 Grain	2 slices whole-wheat bread	2 Grain	2 slices whole-wheat bread	2 Grain	2 slices whole-wheat bread	2 Grain
	1 cup raw veggies	1 Vegetable	1 cup raw veggies	1 Vegetable	1 cup raw veggies with 2 tsp low-fat dressing	1 Vegetable	1 cup raw veggies with 2 tsp low-fat dressing	1 Vegetable
Snack	3 squares graham crackers	1 Grain	3 squares graham crackers	1 Grain	6 squares graham crackers with 1 tsp natural peanut butter	2 Grain 0.5 Protein 1 Fat	6 squares graham crackers with 1 tsp natural peanut butter	2 Grain 0.5 Protein 1 Fat
	4 ounces nonfat milk	0.5 Milk	4 ounces nonfat milk	0.5 Milk	8 ounces nonfat milk	1 Milk	8 ounces nonfat milk	1 Milk

Dinner							
Chicken Breast Veronique (page 91)	3 Protein 2 Fat	Chicken Breast Veronique (page 91)	3 Protein 2 Fat	Chicken Breast Veronique (page 91)	3 Protein 2 Fat	Chicken Breast Veronique (page 91)	3 Protein 2 Fat
½ cup brown rice	1 Grain	½ cup brown rice	1 Grain	1 cup brown rice	2 Grain	1 cup brown rice	2 Grain
Roasted Asparagus with Parmesan (page 143)	2 Vegetable 0.2 Fat	Roasted Asparagus with Parmesan (page 143)	2 Vegetable 0.2 Fat	Roasted Asparagus with Parmesan (page 143)	2 Vegetable 0.2 Fat	Roasted Asparagus with Parmesan (page 143)	2 Vegetable 0.2 Fat
4 ounces nonfat yogurt	0.5 Milk	4 ounces nonfat yogurt	0.5 Milk	8 ounces nonfat yogurt	1 Milk	8 ounces nonfat yogurt	1 Milk
1 cup strawberries	1 Fruit	1 cup strawberries	1 Fruit	1½ cups strawberries	1.5 Fruit	1½ cups strawberries	1.5 Fruit
				¼ cup nuts	1 Protein 2 Fat	¼ cup nuts	1 Protein 2 Fat
Food group totals	4 Grain 4.8 Protein 2 Milk 2 Fruit 3 Vegetable 2.4 Fat		5 Grain 4.8 Protein 2 Milk 2 Fruit 3 Vegetable 2.4 Fat		8 Grain 6.3 Protein 3 Milk 2.5 Fruit 3 Vegetable 5.7 Fat		8 Grain 6.3 Protein 3 Milk 2.5 Fruit 3 Vegetable 5.7 Fat

WEEK 1

Day 2	1,200 Calories Foods	Food group servings	1,500 Calories Foods	Food group servings	1,800 Calories Foods	Food group servings	2,200 Calories Foods	Food group servings
Breakfast	Classic Orange Julius (page 69)	0.5 Milk 3 Fruit	Classic Orange Julius (page 69)	0.5 Milk 3 Fruit	Classic Orange Julius (page 69)	0.5 Milk 3 Fruit	Classic Orange Julius (page 69)	0.5 Milk 3 Fruit
	½ English muffin, 1 Tbsp low-fat cheese	1 Grain 1 Fat	½ English muffin, 1 Tbsp low-fat cheese	1 Grain 1 Fat	1 English muffin, 1 Tbsp low-fat cream cheese	2 Grain 1 Fat	1 English muffin, 1 Tbsp low-fat cream cheese	2 Grain 1 Fat
Snack	8 ounces low-fat yogurt	1 Milk	8 ounces low-fat yogurt	1 Milk	8 ounces low-fat yogurt	1 Milk	8 ounces low-fat yogurt	1 Milk
	1 cup raw veggies	1 Vegetable	1 cup raw veggies	1 Vegetable	1 cup raw veggies	1 Vegetable	1 cup raw veggies with 1 Tbsp low-fat dressing	1 Vegetable 1 Fat
							3 Tbsp GrapeNuts	1 Grain
Lunch	Open-face grilled cheese: 1 slice whole-wheat toast, 1 tsp Smart Balance Buttery Spread, 1 ounce low-fat cheese, 2 slices tomato	1 Grain 1 Protein 1 Fat	Grilled cheese sandwich: 2 slices whole-wheat toast, 1 tsp Smart Balance Buttery Spread, 2 ounces low-fat cheese, 2 slices tomato	2 Grain 2 Protein 1 Fat	Grilled cheese sandwich: 2 slices whole-wheat toast, 1 tsp Smart Balance Buttery Spread, 2 ounces low-fat cheese, 2 slices tomato	2 Grain 2 Protein 1 Fat	Grilled cheese sandwich: 2 slices whole-wheat toast, 1 tsp Smart Balance Buttery Spread, 2 ounces low-fat cheese, 2 slices tomato	2 Grain 2 Protein 1 Fat
	4 ounces nonfat milk	0.5 Milk	8 ounces nonfat milk	1 Milk	12 ounces nonfat milk	1.5 Milk	12 ounces nonfat milk	1.5 Milk

	Plan 1		Plan 2		Plan 3		Plan 4	
Snack	1 cup carrot sticks	1 Vegetable	1 cup carrot sticks	1 Vegetable	½ cup low-fat cottage cheese	2 Protein	¾ cup low-fat cottage cheese	3 Protein
					1 cup melon cubes	1 Fruit	1 cup melon cubes	1 Fruit
					1 cup carrot sticks	1 Vegetable	1 cup carrot sticks	1 Vegetable
					4 slices Melba toast	1 Grain	4 slices Melba toast	1 Grain
Dinner	Beef Roast Excellente (page 107)	2.5 Protein 2 Grain 1 Fat	Beef Roast Excellente (page 107)	2.5 Protein 2 Grain 1 Fat	Beef Roast Excellente (page 107)	2.5 Protein 2 Grain 1 Fat	Beef Roast Excellente (page 107)	2.5 Protein 2 Grain 1 Fat
	Orange Ginger-Glazed Carrots (page 148)	1.5 Vegetable	Orange Ginger-Glazed Carrots (page 148)	1.5 Vegetable	Orange Ginger-Glazed Carrots (page 148)	1.5 Vegetable	Orange Ginger-Glazed Carrots (page 148)	1.5 Vegetable
			1 small whole-wheat roll with 1 tsp Smart Balance Buttery Spread	1 Grain 1 Fat	1 small whole-wheat roll with 1 tsp Smart Balance Buttery Spread	1 Grain 1 Fat	1 small whole-wheat roll with 1 tsp Smart Balance Buttery Spread	1 Grain 1 Fat
	½ cup sugar-free gelatin, 1 Tbsp nonfat nondairy whipped topping	None	½ cup sugar-free gelatin, 1 Tbsp nonfat nondairy whipped topping	None	½ cup sugar-free gelatin, 1 Tbsp nonfat nondairy whipped topping	None	½ cup sugar-free gelatin, 1 Tbsp nonfat nondairy whipped topping	None
Food group totals		4 Grain 4.5 Protein 2 Milk 3 Fruit 3.5 Vegetable 2 Fat		6 Grain 4.5 Protein 2.5 Milk 3 Fruit 3.5 Vegetable 4 Fat		8 Grain 6.5 Protein 2.5 Milk 5 Fruit 3.5 Vegetable 4 Fat		9 Grain 7.5 Protein 3 Milk 4 Fruit 3.5 Vegetable 5 Fat

WEEK 1	1,200 Calories		1,500 Calories		1,800 Calories		2,200 Calories	
Day 3	Foods	Food group servings	Foods	Food group servings	Foods	Food group servings	Foods	Food group servings
Breakfast	½ cup oatmeal	1 Grain	½ cup oatmeal	1 Grain	½ cup oatmeal	1 Grain	½ cup oatmeal	1 Grain
	½ grapefruit	1 Fruit	½ grapefruit	1 Fruit	½ grapefruit	1 Fruit	½ grapefruit	1 Fruit
	8 ounces nonfat milk	1 Milk	8 ounces nonfat milk	1 Milk	12 ounces nonfat milk	1.5 Milk	12 ounces nonfat milk	1.5 Milk
					1 slice raisin toast with 1 Tbsp low-fat cream cheese	1 Grain / 1 Fat	1 slice raisin toast with 1 Tbsp low-fat cream cheese	1 Grain / 1 Fat
Snack	½ cup edamame	0.5 Vegetable	½ cup edamame	0.5 Vegetable	½ cup edamame	0.5 Vegetable	½ cup edamame	0.5 Vegetable
			1 hard-boiled egg	1 Protein	1 hard-boiled egg	1 Protein	1 hard-boiled egg	1 Protein
Lunch	Chicken Pita Pockets (page 50)	1 Grain / 2 Protein / 0.2 Vegetable / 1.4 Fat	Chicken Pita Pockets (page 50)	1 Grain / 2 Protein / 0.2 Vegetable / 1.4 Fat	Chicken Pita Pockets (page 50)	1 Grain / 2 Protein / 0.2 Vegetable / 1.4 Fat	Chicken Pita Pockets (page 50)	1 Grain / 2 Protein / 0.2 Vegetable / 1.4 Fat
	1 cup cut-up celery and carrots	1 Vegetable	1 cup cut-up celery and carrots	1 Vegetable	1 cup cut-up celery and carrots	1 Vegetable	1 cup cut-up celery and carrots	1 Vegetable
	8 ounces nonfat milk	1 Milk	8 ounces nonfat milk	1 Milk	8 ounces nonfat milk	1 Milk	8 ounces nonfat milk	1 Milk
	1 apple	1 Fruit	1 apple	1 Fruit	1 apple	1 Fruit	1 apple	1 Fruit
Snack	3 cups air-popped or microwave light popcorn	1 Grain	3 cups air-popped or microwave light popcorn	1 Grain	3 cups air-popped or microwave light popcorn	1 Grain	3 cups air-popped or microwave light popcorn	1 Grain

	Dinner		Food group totals
Plan 1	½ serving Turkey Taco Salad (page 84)	0.25 Grain / 2.5 Protein / 0.5 Vegetable / 0.6 Fat	4.25 Grain / 4.5 Protein / 2 Milk / 3 Fruit / 2.2 Vegetable / 2 Fat
	½ cup brown rice	1 Grain	
	Frozen 100% fruit juice bar	1 Fruit	
Plan 2	½ serving Turkey Taco Salad (page 84)	0.25 Grain / 2.5 Protein / 0.5 Vegetable / 0.6 Fat	5.25 Grain / 5.5 Protein / 2 Milk / 3 Fruit / 2.2 Vegetable / 2 Fat
	1 cup brown rice	2 Grain	
	Frozen 100% fruit juice bar	1 Fruit	
Plan 3	Turkey Taco Salad (page 84)	0.5 Grain / 5 Protein / 1 Vegetable / 1.2 Fat	8.5 Grain / 8 Protein / 2.5 Milk / 3 Fruit / 2.7 Vegetable / 4.6 Fat
	2 cups brown rice with 1 tsp Smart Balance Buttery Spread	4 Grain / 1 Fat	
	Frozen 100% fruit juice bar	1 Fruit	
Plan 4	Turkey Taco Salad (page 84)	0.5 Grain / 5 Protein / 1 Vegetable / 1.2 Fat	8.5 Grain / 8 Protein / 2.5 Milk / 3 Fruit / 2.7 Vegetable / 4.6 Fat
	2 cups brown rice with 1 tsp Smart Balance Buttery Spread	4 Grain / 1 Fat	
	Frozen 100% fruit juice bar	1 Fruit	

WEEK 1 Day 4	1,200 Calories Foods	Food group servings	1,500 Calories Foods	Food group servings	1,800 Calories Foods	Food group servings	2,200 Calories Foods	Food group servings
Breakfast	Fruit and Yogurt Parfait (page 65) or small McDonald's parfait	1 Grain 0.5 Fruit 0.5 Milk 0.4 Fat	Fruit and Yogurt Parfait (page 65) or small McDonald's parfait	1 Grain 0.5 Fruit 0.5 Milk 0.4 Fat	Fruit and Yogurt Parfait (page 65) or small McDonald's parfait	1 Grain 0.5 Fruit 0.5 Milk 0.4 Fat	Fruit and Yogurt Parfait (page 65) or small McDonald's parfait	1 Grain 0.5 Fruit 0.5 Milk 0.4 Fat
					1 whole-wheat bagel with 2 tsp all-fruit jelly	2 Grain	1 whole-wheat bagel with 1 Tbsp low-fat cream cheese	2 Grain 1 Fat
Snack	1 small low-fat granola bar	1 Grain	1 small low-fat granola bar	1 Grain	1 small low-fat granola bar	1 Grain	2 small low-fat granola bars	2 Grain
	8 ounces nonfat milk	1 Milk	8 ounces nonfat milk	1 Milk	8 ounces nonfat milk	1 Milk	8 ounces nonfat milk	1 Milk
Lunch	½ serving Turkey Taco Salad (page 84)	0.25 Grain 2.5 Protein 0.5 Vegetable 0.6 Fat	½ serving Turkey Taco Salad (page 84)	0.25 Grain 2.5 Protein 0.5 Vegetable 0.6 Fat	Turkey Taco Salad (page 84)	0.5 Grain 5 Protein 1 Vegetable 1.2 Fat	Turkey Taco Salad (page 84)	0.5 Grain 5 Protein 1 Vegetable 1.2 Fat
	Baked Tortilla Chips (page 62)	1.3 Grain 0.8 Fat	2 servings Baked Tortilla Chips (page 62)	2.6 Grain 1.6 Fat	2 servings Baked Tortilla Chips (page 62)	2.6 Grain 1.6 Fat	2 servings Baked Tortilla Chips (page 62)	2.6 Grain 1.6 Fat
	8 ounces nonfat milk	1 Milk	8 ounces nonfat milk	1 Milk	12 ounces nonfat milk	1.5 Milk	12 ounces nonfat milk	1.5 Milk
Snack	½ cup no-sugar-added applesauce	1 Fruit	½ cup no-sugar-added applesauce	1 Fruit	½ cup no-sugar-added applesauce	1 Fruit	½ cup no-sugar-added applesauce	1 Fruit

	Food	Amounts	Food	Amounts	Food	Amounts	Food	Amounts
Dinner	1 cup raw cut-up veggies	1 Vegetable	1 cup raw cut-up veggies with 1 Tbsp low-fat dressing	1 Vegetable 1 Fat	1 cup raw cut-up veggies with 1 Tbsp low-fat dressing	1 Vegetable 1 Fat	1 cup raw cut-up veggies with 1 Tbsp low-fat dressing	1 Vegetable 1 Fat
	Tamale Pie (page 93)	1 Grain 1 Vegetable 1.5 Protein 0.8 Fat	Tamale Pie (page 93)	1 Grain 1 Vegetable 1.5 Protein 0.8 Fat	1¼ servings Tamale Pie (page 93)	1.25 Grain 1.25 Vegetable 1.9 Protein 1 Fat	1½ servings Tamale Pie (page 93)	1.5 Grain 1.5 Vegetable 2.25 Protein 1.2 Fat
	1 cup salad with Thousand Island Dressing (page 165)	1 Vegetable 0.1 Protein 0.1 Fat	1 cup salad with Thousand Island Dressing (page 165)	1 Vegetable 0.1 Protein 0.1 Fat	1 cup salad with Thousand Island Dressing (page 165)	1 Vegetable 0.1 Protein 0.1 Fat	1 cup salad with Thousand Island Dressing (page 165)	1 Vegetable 0.1 Protein 0.1 Fat
	4 ounces tomato juice	1 Vegetable	4 ounces tomato juice	1 Vegetable	4 ounces tomato juice	1 Vegetable	4 ounces tomato juice	1 Vegetable
	Oven-Roasted Fruit (page 64)	1 Fruit	Oven-Roasted Fruit (page 64)	1 Fruit	1½ servings Oven-Roasted Fruit (page 64)	1.5 Fruit	1½ servings Oven-Roasted Fruit (page 64)	1.5 Fruit
Food group totals		4.55 Grain 4.4 Protein 2.5 Milk 2.3 Fruit 4.5 Vegetable 2.6 Fat		5.85 Grain 4.4 Protein 2.5 Milk 2.5 Fruit 4.5 Vegetable 4.8 Fat		8.35 Grain 7.3 Protein 3 Milk 3 Fruit 5.25 Vegetable 5.8 Fat		9.6 Grain 7.65 Protein 3 Milk 3 Fruit 5.5 Vegetable 6.8 Fat

Day 5	1,200 Calories		1,500 Calories		1,800 Calories		2,200 Calories	
	Foods	Food group servings	Foods	Food group servings	Foods	Food group servings	Foods	Food group servings
Breakfast	¾ cup Cheerios	1 Grain	¾ cup Cheerios	1 Grain	¾ cup Cheerios	1 Grain	1½ cups Cheerios	2 Grain
	8 ounces nonfat milk	1 Milk	8 ounces nonfat milk	1 Milk	12 ounces nonfat milk	1.5 Milk	16 ounces nonfat milk	2 Milk
	1 cup berries	1 Fruit	1 cup berries	1 Fruit	1 cup berries	1 Fruit	1 cup berries	1 Fruit
Snack	1 cup edamame	1 Vegetable	1 cup edamame	1 Vegetable	1 cup edamame	1 Vegetable	1 cup edamame	1 Vegetable
					6 low-fat wheat crackers	1 Grain	6 low-fat wheat crackers with 1 tsp Smart Balance Buttery Spread	1 Grain 1 Fat
					1 ounce low-fat string cheese or ¼ cup low-fat cottage cheese	1 Protein	1 ounce low-fat string cheese or ¼ cup low-fat cottage cheese	1 Protein
Lunch	Sandwich: 2 slices whole-wheat bread, 1 Tbsp natural peanut butter, 1 Tbsp all-fruit jelly	2 Grain 0.5 Protein 1 Fat	Sandwich: 2 slices whole-wheat bread, 1 Tbsp natural peanut butter, 1 Tbsp all-fruit jelly	2 Grain 0.5 Protein 1 Fat	Sandwich: 2 slices whole-wheat bread, 1 Tbsp natural peanut butter, 1 Tbsp all-fruit jelly	2 Grain 0.5 Protein 1 Fat	Sandwich: 2 slices whole-wheat bread, 1 Tbsp natural peanut butter, 1 Tbsp all-fruit jelly	2 Grain 0.5 Protein 1 Fat
	8 ounces nonfat yogurt	1 Milk	8 ounces nonfat yogurt	1 Milk	8 ounces nonfat yogurt	1 Milk	8 ounces nonfat yogurt with ¼ cup nuts	1 Milk 1 Protein 2 Fat

	Food	Amount	Food	Amount	Food	Amount	Food	Amount
Snack	1 cup sliced fruit	1 Fruit	1 cup sliced fruit	1 Fruit	1 cup sliced fruit	1 Fruit	1 cup sliced fruit	1 Fruit
					2 rice cakes		2 rice cakes	1 Grain
Dinner	½ serving Shrimp and Corn Wraps (page 100)	1 Grain 2 Protein 0.5 Fat	Shrimp and Corn Wraps (page 100)	2 Grain 4 Protein 1 Fat	Shrimp and Corn Wraps (page 100)	2 Grain 4 Protein 1 Fat	1½ servings Shrimp and Corn Wrap (page 100)	3 Grain 6 Protein 1.5 Fat
	1 cup steamed zucchini	1 Vegetable	1 cup steamed zucchini	1 Vegetable	1 cup steamed zucchini	1 Vegetable	1 cup steamed zucchini	1 Vegetable
	1 cup pineapple	1 Fruit	1 cup pineapple	1 Fruit	1 cup pineapple	1 Fruit	1 cup pineapple	1 Fruit
	½ serving Vanilla Pudding (page 189)	0.5 Protein 0.2 Fat 0.25 Milk	Vanilla Pudding (page 189)	1 Protein 0.4 Fat 0.5 Milk	Vanilla Pudding (page 189)	1 Protein 0.4 Fat 0.5 Milk	Vanilla Pudding (page 189)	1 Protein 0.4 Fat 0.5 Milk
	8 animal crackers	1 Grain	8 animal crackers	1 Grain	8 animal crackers	1 Grain	8 animal crackers	1 Grain
Food group totals		5 Grain 3 Protein 2.25 Milk 3 Fruit 2 Vegetable 1.7 Fat		6 Grain 5.5 Protein 2.5 Milk 3 Fruit 2 Vegetable 2.4 Fat		8 Grain 6.5 Protein 2.5 Milk 3 Fruit 2 Vegetable 3.4 Fat		10 Grain 9.5 Protein 3.5 Milk 3 Fruit 2 Vegetable 5.9 Fat

WEEK 1

Day 6

	1,200 Calories		1,500 Calories		1,800 Calories		2,200 Calories	
	Foods	Food group servings	Foods	Food group servings	Foods	Food group servings	Foods	Food group servings
Breakfast	Egg 'n' Ham Breakfast Sandwich (page 27)	3.4 Protein 2 Grain 0.1 Milk 2.2 Fat	Egg 'n' Ham Breakfast Sandwich (page 27)	3.4 Protein 2 Grain 0.1 Milk 2.2 Fat	Egg 'n' Ham Breakfast Sandwich (page 27)	3.4 Protein 2 Grain 0.1 Milk 2.2 Fat	Egg 'n' Ham Breakfast Sandwich (page 27)	3.4 Protein 2 Grain 0.1 Milk 2.2 Fat
	12 grapes	1 Fruit	12 grapes	1 Fruit	18 grapes	1.5 Fruit	24 grapes	2 Fruit
Snack	Kicked-up Hot Chocolate (page 68)	0.5 Milk 0.2 Fat	Kicked-up Hot Chocolate (page 68)	0.5 Milk 0.2 Fat	Kicked-up Hot Chocolate (page 68)	0.5 Milk 0.2 Fat	Kicked-up Hot Chocolate (page 68)	0.5 Milk 0.2 Fat
Lunch	1 veggie burger	1 Protein 0.5 Grain	2 veggie burgers	2 Protein 1 Grain	2 veggie burgers	2 Protein 1 Grain	2 veggie burgers	2 Protein 1 Grain
	Grilled mushrooms and onions	0.5 Vegetable	Grilled mushrooms and onions	0.5 Vegetable	Grilled mushrooms and onions	0.5 Vegetable	Grilled mushrooms and onions	0.5 Vegetable
	1 pear	1 Fruit	1 pear	1 Fruit	1 pear	1 Fruit	1 pear	1 Fruit
	6 ounces nonfat milk	0.75 Milk	6 ounces nonfat milk	0.75 Milk	8 ounces nonfat milk	1 Milk	8 ounces nonfat milk	1 Milk
					1 ounce low-fat cheese	1 Protein	1 ounce low-fat cheese	1 Protein
							⅛ avocado	1 Fat
Snack	2 stalks celery with 1 tsp natural peanut butter	1 Vegetable 0.1 Protein 0.3 Fat	2 stalks celery with 1 Tbsp natural peanut butter	1 Vegetable 0.5 Protein 1 Fat	2 stalks celery with 1 Tbsp natural peanut butter	1 Vegetable 0.5 Protein 1 Fat	2 stalks celery with 1 Tbsp natural peanut butter	1 Vegetable 0.5 Protein 1 Fat

Dinner	4 ounces nonfat milk	0.5 Milk	4 ounces nonfat milk	0.5 Milk	8 ounces nonfat milk	1 Milk	8 ounces nonfat milk	1 Milk
	½ serving Indian Vegetable Curry (page 104)	1.5 Grain 0.38 Vegetable 0.65 Fat	½ serving Indian Vegetable Curry (page 104)	1.5 Grain 0.38 Vegetable 0.65 Fat	Indian Vegetable Curry (page 104)	3 Grain 0.75 Vegetable 1.3 Fat	Indian Vegetable Curry (page 104)	3 Grain 0.75 Vegetable 1.3 Fat
	1 cup salad	1 Vegetable	1 cup salad with 1 Tbsp low-fat dressing	1 Vegetable 1 Fat	1 cup salad with 1 Tbsp low-fat dressing	1 Vegetable 1 Fat	1 cup salad with 2 Tbsp low-fat dressing	1 Vegetable 2 Fat
	Strawberry Shortcake (page 181)	1 Grain 0.75 Fruit 1.6 Fat	Strawberry Shortcake (page 181)	1 Grain 0.75 Fruit 1.6 Fat	Strawberry Shortcake (page 181)	1 Grain 0.75 Fruit 1.6 Fat	Strawberry Shortcake (page 181)	1 Grain 0.75 Fruit 1.6 Fat
	6 ounces nonfat milk	0.75 Milk	6 ounces nonfat milk	0.75 Milk	8 ounces nonfat milk	1 Milk	8 ounces nonfat milk	1 Milk
	½ cup light ice cream or nonfat frozen yogurt	1 Fat	½ cup light ice cream or nonfat frozen yogurt	1 Fat	½ cup light ice cream or nonfat frozen yogurt	1 Fat	½ cup light ice cream or nonfat frozen yogurt	1 Fat
Food group totals		5 Grain 4.5 Protein 2.6 Milk 2.75 Fruit 2.88 Vegetable 5.95 Fat		5.5 Grain 5.9 Protein 2.6 Milk 2.75 Fruit 2.88 Vegetable 7.65 Fat		7 Grain 6.9 Protein 3.6 Milk 3.25 Fruit 3.25 Vegetable 8.3 Fat		7 Grain 6.9 Protein 3.6 Milk 3.75 Fruit 3.25 Vegetable 10.3 Fat

	1,200 Calories		1,500 Calories		1,800 Calories		2,200 Calories	
Day 7	Foods	Food group servings	Foods	Food group servings	Foods	Food group servings	Foods	Food group servings
Breakfast	2 Whole-Wheat Blueberry Pancakes (page 32)	1.5 Grain 0.2 Fruit 0.2 Milk 0.1 Protein 0.6 Fat	2 Whole-Wheat Blueberry Pancakes (page 32)	1.5 Grain 0.2 Fruit 0.2 Milk 0.1 Protein 0.6 Fat	3 Whole-Wheat Blueberry Pancakes (page 32) with 1 tsp Smart Balance Buttery Spread	2.3 Grain 0.3 Fruit 0.3 Milk 0.2 Protein 1.9 Fat	3 Whole-Wheat Blueberry Pancakes (page 32) with 1 tsp Smart Balance Buttery Spread	2.3 Grain 0.3 Fruit 0.3 Milk 0.2 Protein 1.9 Fat
	8 ounces nonfat milk	1 Milk	8 ounces nonfat milk	1 Milk	8 ounces nonfat milk	1 Milk	8 ounces nonfat milk	1 Milk
Snack	Individual Apple Crumble (page 185)	0.5 Grain 1.6 Fruit 0.2 Fat	Individual Apple Crumble (page 185)	0.5 Grain 1.6 Fruit 0.2 Fat	Individual Apple Crumble (page 185)	0.5 Grain 1.6 Fruit 0.2 Fat	Individual Apple Crumble (page 185)	0.5 Grain 1.6 Fruit 0.2 Fat
					8 ounces nonfat yogurt	1 Milk	8 ounces nonfat yogurt	1 Milk
					1 orange	1 Fruit	1 orange	1 Fruit
							½ cup low-fat granola	2 Grain 2 Fat
Lunch	Sandwich: 2 ounces lean turkey, 1 slice whole-wheat toast, mustard, lettuce, tomato	2 Protein 1 Grain	Sandwich: 2 ounces lean turkey, 2 slices whole-wheat toast, mustard, lettuce, tomato	2 Protein 2 Grain	Sandwich: 2 ounces lean turkey, 2 slices whole-wheat toast, mustard, lettuce, tomato	2 Protein 2 Grain	Sandwich: 2 ounces lean turkey, 2 slices whole-wheat toast, mustard, lettuce, tomato	2 Protein 2 Grain
	1 cup salad	1 Vegetable	1 cup salad with 1 Tbsp low-fat dressing	1 Vegetable 1 Fat	1 cup salad with 1 Tbsp low-fat dressing	1 Vegetable 1 Fat	1 cup salad with 1 Tbsp low-fat dressing	1 Vegetable 1 Fat

Snack	½ cup raw vegetable	0.5 Vegetable	1 cup raw vegetable	1 Vegetable	1 small banana	1 Fruit	1 small banana	1 Fruit
					1 cup raw vegetable	1 Vegetable	1 cup raw vegetable	1 Vegetable
					½ whole-wheat pita with 1½ Tbsp hummus	1 Grain / 1 Fat	½ whole-wheat pita with 1½ Tbsp hummus	1 Grain / 1 Fat
Dinner	3 ounces Sweet-Spicy Glazed Salmon (page 98)	2.5 Protein / 1 Fat	3 ounces Sweet-Spicy Glazed Salmon (page 98)	2.5 Protein / 1 Fat	4 ounces Sweet-Spicy Glazed Salmon (page 98)	3.3 Protein / 1.3 Fat	4 ounces Sweet-Spicy Glazed Salmon (page 98)	3.3 Protein / 1.3 Fat
	½ cup steamed broccoli	0.5 Vegetable	1 cup steamed broccoli	1 Vegetable	1 cup steamed broccoli	1 Vegetable	1½ cups steamed broccoli	1.5 Vegetable
	½ cup brown rice	1 Grain	½ cup brown rice	1 Grain	1 cup brown rice	2 Grain	1 cup brown rice	2 Grain
	8 ounces nonfat milk	1 Milk	8 ounces nonfat milk	1 Milk	8 ounces nonfat milk	1 Milk	8 ounces nonfat milk	1 Milk
Food group totals		4 Grain / 4.6 Protein / 2.2 Milk / 1.8 Fruit / 2 Vegetable / 1.8 Fat		5 Grain / 4.6 Protein / 2.2 Milk / 1.8 Fruit / 3 Vegetable / 2.8 Fat		7.8 Grain / 5.5 Protein / 3.3 Milk / 3.9 Fruit / 3 Vegetable / 5.4 Fat		9.8 Grain / 5.5 Protein / 3.3 Milk / 3.9 Fruit / 3.5 Vegetable / 7.4 Fat

Day 1	1,200 Calories		1,500 Calories		1,800 Calories		2,200 Calories	
	Foods	Food group servings	Foods	Food group servings	Foods	Food group servings	Foods	Food group servings
Breakfast	½ cup oatmeal	1 Grain	1 cup oatmeal	2 Grain	1 cup oatmeal	2 Grain	1 cup oatmeal	2 Grain
	¼ cup raisins	1 Fruit	¼ cup raisins	1 Fruit	¼ cup raisins	1 Fruit	¼ cup raisins	1 Fruit
	8 ounces nonfat milk	1 Milk	8 ounces nonfat milk	1 Milk	16 ounces nonfat milk	2 Milk	16 ounces nonfat milk	2 Milk
Snack	1 apple	1 Fruit	1 apple with 1½ tsp natural peanut butter	1 Fruit 0.25 Protein 0.5 Fat	1 apple with 1½ tsp natural peanut butter	1 Fruit 0.25 Protein 0.5 Fat	1 apple with 1½ tsp natural peanut butter	1 Fruit 0.25 Protein 0.5 Fat
					2 rice cakes	1 Grain	2 rice cakes	1 Grain
Lunch	Spiral Pinwheel Sandwich (page 42)	1 Grain 0.25 Vegetable 0.16 Fruit 2 Protein 0.8 Fat	Spiral Pinwheel Sandwich (page 42)	1 Grain 0.25 Vegetable 0.16 Fruit 2 Protein 0.8 Fat	Spiral Pinwheel Sandwich (page 42)	1 Grain 0.25 Vegetable 0.16 Fruit 2 Protein 0.8 Fat	Spiral Pinwheel Sandwich (page 42)	1 Grain 0.25 Vegetable 0.16 Fruit 2 Protein 0.8 Fat
	1 cup raw veggies	1 Vegetable	1 cup raw veggies	1 Vegetable	2 cups raw veggies	2 Vegetable	2 cups raw veggies with 1 Tbsp low-fat dressing	2 Vegetable 1 Fat
					10 pretzels	1 Grain	10 pretzels	1 Grain

Snack	Baked Vegetable Quesadillas (page 56)	0.5 Grain 0.5 Vegetable 0.3 Protein 0.4 Fat	Baked Vegetable Quesadillas (page 56)	0.5 Grain 0.5 Vegetable 0.3 Protein 0.4 Fat	Baked Vegetable Quesadillas (page 56)	0.5 Grain 0.5 Vegetable 0.3 Protein 0.4 Fat	2 servings Baked Vegetable Quesadillas (page 56) with 1 Tbsp low-fat sour cream	1 Grain 1 Vegetable 0.6 Protein 1.3 Fat
	4 ounces nonfat milk	0.5 Milk	4 ounces nonfat milk	0.5 Milk	8 ounces nonfat milk	1 Milk	8 ounces nonfat milk	1 Milk
Dinner	Macaroni and Cheese (page 121)	2.5 Grain 0.5 Milk 2.5 Protein 1.4 Fat	Macaroni and Cheese (page 121)	2.5 Grain 0.5 Milk 2.5 Protein 1.4 Fat	Macaroni and Cheese (page 121)	2.5 Grain 0.5 Milk 2.5 Protein 1.4 Fat	Macaroni and Cheese (page 121)	2.5 Grain 0.5 Milk 2.5 Protein 1.4 Fat
	1 cup salad with 1 Tbsp low-fat dressing	1 Vegetable 1 Fat	1 cup salad with 2 Tbsp low-fat dressing	1 Vegetable 2 Fat	1 cup salad with 2 Tbsp low-fat dressing	1 Vegetable 2 Fat	1 cup salad with 2 Tbsp low-fat dressing	1 Vegetable 2 Fat
	Chilled Strawberry Soup (page 66)	0.5 Fruit 0.3 Milk 0.2 Fat	Chilled Strawberry Soup (page 66)	0.5 Fruit 0.3 Milk 0.2 Fat	Chilled Strawberry Soup (page 66)	0.5 Fruit 0.3 Milk 0.2 Fat	1½ servings Chilled Strawberry Soup (page 66)	0.75 Fruit 0.45 Milk 0.3 Fat
Food group totals		5 Grain 4.8 Protein 2.3 Milk 2.66 Fruit 2.75 Vegetable 3.8 Fat		6 Grain 5.05 Protein 2.8 Milk 2.66 Fruit 2.75 Vegetable 5.3 Fat		8 Grain 5.05 Protein 3.8 Milk 2.66 Fruit 3.75 Vegetable 5.3 Fat		6.7 Grain 5.35 Protein 3.95 Milk 2.91 Fruit 4.25 Vegetable 7.3 Fat

WEEK 2	1,200 Calories		1,500 Calories		1,800 Calories		2,200 Calories	
Day 2	Foods	Food group servings	Foods	Food group servings	Foods	Food group servings	Foods	Food group servings
Breakfast	1 whole-wheat bagel, toasted with 1 slice low-fat cheese	2 Grain 1 Protein	1 whole-wheat bagel, toasted with 2 slices low-fat cheese	2 Grain 2 Protein	1 whole-wheat bagel, toasted with 2 slices low-fat cheese	2 Grain 2 Protein	1 whole-wheat bagel, toasted with 2 slices low-fat cheese	2 Grain 2 Protein
	4 ounces nonfat milk	0.5 Milk	6 ounces nonfat milk	0.75 Milk	12 ounces nonfat milk	1.5 Milk	12 ounces nonfat milk	1.5 Milk
Snack	1 low-fat granola bar	1 Grain	1 low-fat granola bar	1 Grain	2 low-fat granola bars	2 Grain	2 low-fat granola bars	2 Grain
Lunch	Inside-Out Turkey Sandwich (page 41)	1 Grain 3 Protein 1.4 Fat	Inside-Out Turkey Sandwich (page 41)	1 Grain 3 Protein 1.4 Fat	Inside-Out Turkey Sandwich (page 41)	1 Grain 3 Protein 1.4 Fat	Inside-Out Turkey Sandwich (page 41)	1 Grain 3 Protein 1.4 Fat
	1 cup raw carrots	1 Vegetable	1 cup raw carrots	1 Vegetable	1 cup raw carrots	1 Vegetable	1 cup raw carrots, 1 cup celery	2 Vegetable
	¼ cup raisins	1 Fruit	¼ cup raisins	1 Fruit	¼ cup raisins	1 Fruit	¼ cup raisins	1 Fruit
Snack	Peanut Butter Delight (page 71)	1 Fruit 0.75 Milk 1.4 Fat	Peanut Butter Delight (page 71)	1 Fruit 0.75 Milk 1.4 Fat	Peanut Butter Delight (page 71)	1 Fruit 0.75 Milk 1.4 Fat	1½ servings Peanut Butter Delight (page 71)	1.5 Fruit 1.1 Milk 2.1 Fat
Dinner	Italian Minestrone Soup (page 132)	0.5 Grain 1 Vegetable 1 Protein	Italian Minestrone Soup (page 132)	0.5 Grain 1 Vegetable 1 Protein	Italian Minestrone Soup (page 132)	0.5 Grain 1 Vegetable 1 Protein	1½ servings Italian Minestrone Soup (page 132)	0.75 Grain 1.5 Vegetable 1.5 Protein

Food	Plan 1		Plan 2		Plan 3		Plan 4	
	1 whole-wheat roll	1 Grain	1 whole-wheat roll with 1 tsp Smart Balance Buttery Spread	1 Grain 1 Fat	2 whole-wheat rolls with 1 tsp Smart Balance Buttery Spread	2 Grain 1 Fat	2 whole-wheat rolls with 1 tsp Smart Balance Buttery Spread	2 Grain 1 Fat
	1 cup salad with 1 Tbsp low-fat dressing	1 Vegetable 1 Fat	1 cup salad with 1 Tbsp low-fat dressing	1 Vegetable 1 Fat	1 cup salad with 1 Tbsp low-fat dressing	1 Vegetable 1 Fat	1 cup salad with 1 Tbsp low-fat dressing	1 Vegetable 1 Fat
	Frozen Fruit Pop (page 65)	1 Fruit 1 Milk	Frozen Fruit Pop (page 65)	1 Fruit 1 Milk	Frozen Fruit Pop (page 65)	1 Fruit 1 Milk	Frozen Fruit Pop (page 65)	1 Fruit 1 Milk
Food group totals	5.5 Grain 5 Protein 2.25 Milk 3 Fruit 3 Vegetable 3.8 Fat		5.5 Grain 6 Protein 2.5 Milk 3 Fruit 3 Vegetable 4.8 Fat		7.5 Grain 6 Protein 3.25 Milk 3 Fruit 3 Vegetable 4.8 Fat		7.75 Grain 6.5 Protein 3.6 Milk 3.5 Fruit 4.5 Vegetable 5.5 Fat	

Day 3	1,200 Calories Foods	Food group servings	1,500 Calories Foods	Food group servings	1,800 Calories Foods	Food group servings	2,200 Calories Foods	Food group servings
Breakfast	1 bialy or slice of whole-wheat toast with 1 Tbsp low-fat cream cheese	1 Grain 1 Fat	1 bialy or slice of whole-wheat toast with 1 Tbsp low-fat cream cheese	1 Grain 1 Fat	1 bialy or slice of whole-wheat toast with 1 Tbsp low-fat cream cheese	1 Grain 1 Fat	1 bialy or slice of whole-wheat toast with 1 Tbsp low-fat cream cheese	1 Grain 1 Fat
	4 ounces nonfat milk	0.5 Milk	4 ounces nonfat milk	0.5 Milk	8 ounces nonfat milk	1 Milk	8 ounces nonfat milk	1 Milk
Snack	1 orange	1 Fruit	1 orange	1 Fruit	1 orange	1 Fruit	2 oranges	2 Fruit
	8 almonds	1 Protein 2 Fat	8 almonds	1 Protein 2 Fat	8 almonds	1 Protein 2 Fat	12 almonds	1.5 Protein 3 Fat
Lunch	Italian Minestrone Soup (page 132)	0.5 Grain 1 Vegetable 1 Protein	Italian Minestrone Soup (page 132)	0.5 Grain 1 Vegetable 1 Protein	Italian Minestrone Soup (page 132)	0.5 Grain 1 Vegetable 1 Protein	1½ servings Italian Minestrone Soup (page 132)	0.75 Grain 1.5 Vegetable 1.5 Protein
	8 ounces nonfat yogurt	1 Milk	8 ounces nonfat yogurt	1 Milk	8 ounces nonfat yogurt	1 Milk	8 ounces nonfat yogurt, 2 Tbsp GrapeNuts	1 Milk 1 Grain
Snack	Crunchy PB in a Wrap (page 39)	1.25 Grain 1.7 Protein 2.4 Fat 0.25 Fruit	Crunchy PB in a Wrap (page 39)	1.25 Grain 1.7 Protein 2.4 Fat 0.25 Fruit	Crunchy PB in a Wrap (page 39)	1.25 Grain 1.7 Protein 2.4 Fat 0.25 Fruit	Crunchy PB in a Wrap (page 39)	1.25 Grain 1.7 Protein 2.4 Fat 0.25 Fruit
	4 ounces nonfat milk	0.5 Milk	4 ounces nonfat milk	0.5 Milk	8 ounces nonfat milk	1 Milk	8 ounces nonfat milk	1 Milk

Dinner		1 cup raw veggies with 1 Tbsp low-fat dressing — 1 Vegetable, 1 Fat	1 cup raw veggies with 1 Tbsp low-fat dressing — 1 Vegetable, 1 Fat	1 cup raw veggies with 1 Tbsp low-fat dressing — 1 Vegetable, 1 Fat
	1 cup whole-wheat pasta — 2 Grain	1½ cups whole-wheat pasta — 3 Grain	2 cups whole-wheat pasta — 4 Grain	2 cups whole-wheat pasta — 4 Grain
	Spaghetti Sauce (page 123) — 1 Vegetable, 1.6 Protein, 1.6 Fat	Spaghetti Sauce (page 123) — 1 Vegetable, 1.6 Protein, 1.6 Fat	Spaghetti Sauce (page 123) — 1 Vegetable, 1.6 Protein, 1.6 Fat	Spaghetti Sauce (page 123) — 1 Vegetable, 1.6 Protein, 1.6 Fat
	1 cup fruit — 1 Fruit	1 cup fruit — 1 Fruit	1 cup fruit — 1 Fruit	1 cup fruit — 1 Fruit
	Chocolate Pudding (page 188) — 0.3 Milk, 0.2 Fat	Chocolate Pudding (page 188) — 0.3 Milk, 0.2 Fat	Chocolate Pudding (page 188) — 0.3 Milk, 0.2 Fat	Chocolate Pudding (page 188) — 0.3 Milk, 0.2 Fat
Food group totals	4.75 Grain, 5.3 Protein, 2.3 Milk, 2 Fruit, 2 Vegetable, 7.2 Fat	5.75 Grain, 5.3 Protein, 2.3 Milk, 2 Fruit, 3 Vegetable, 8.2 Fat	6.75 Grain, 5.3 Protein, 3.3 Milk, 2 Fruit, 3 Vegetable, 8.2 Fat	8 Grain, 6.3 Protein, 3.3 Milk, 3 Fruit, 3.5 Vegetable, 9.2 Fat

Day 4	1,200 Calories		1,500 Calories		1,800 Calories		2,200 Calories	
	Foods	Food group servings	Foods	Food group servings	Foods	Food group servings	Foods	Food group servings
Breakfast	¼ cup egg substitute	1 Protein	¼ cup egg substitute	1 Protein	¼ cup egg substitute	1 Protein	¼ cup egg substitute	1 Protein
	1 slice whole-wheat toast with 1 Tbsp all-fruit jelly	1 Grain	1 slice whole-wheat toast with 1 Tbsp all-fruit jelly	1 Grain	2 slices whole-wheat toast with 1 Tbsp all-fruit jelly	2 Grain	3 slices whole-wheat toast with 1 Tbsp all-fruit jelly	3 Grain
Snack	½ cup sliced tomato	1 Vegetable	½ cup sliced tomato	1 Vegetable	½ cup sliced tomato	1 Vegetable	½ cup sliced tomato	1 Vegetable
Lunch	Pizza Rolls (page 46)	1 Grain 1.4 Protein 1.4 Vegetable 1.8 Fat	Pizza Rolls (page 46)	1 Grain 1.4 Protein 1.4 Vegetable 1.8 Fat	Pizza Rolls (page 46)	1 Grain 1.4 Protein 1.4 Vegetable 1.8 Fat	Pizza Rolls (page 46)	1 Grain 1.4 Protein 1.4 Vegetable 1.8 Fat
	1 cup pea pods	1 Vegetable	1 cup pea pods	1 Vegetable	1 cup pea pods	1 Vegetable	1 cup pea pods	1 Vegetable
	6 ounces nonfat milk	0.75 Milk	6 ounces nonfat milk	0.75 Milk	8 ounces nonfat milk	1 Milk	8 ounces nonfat milk	1 Milk
					1 pear	1 Fruit	1 pear	1 Fruit
Snack	8 ounces nonfat yogurt	1 Milk	8 ounces nonfat yogurt	1 Milk	8 ounces nonfat yogurt	1 Milk	8 ounces nonfat yogurt	1 Milk
	1 cup melon	1 Fruit	1 cup melon	1 Fruit	1 cup melon	1 Fruit	1 cup melon	1 Fruit
Dinner	Tuna Noodle Casserole (page 118)	1.5 Grain 0.2 Milk 2 Protein 0.6 Fat	1¼ servings Tuna Noodle Casserole (page 118)	1.9 Grain 0.25 Milk 2.5 Protein 0.8 Fat	1½ servings Tuna Noodle Casserole (page 118)	2.3 Grain 0.3 Milk 3 Protein 0.9 Fat	1½ servings Tuna Noodle Casserole (page 118)	2.3 Grain 0.3 Milk 3 Protein 0.9 Fat

1 cup salad with 1 Tbsp low-fat dressing	1 Vegetable 1 Fat	1 cup salad with 1 Tbsp low-fat dressing	1 Vegetable 1 Fat	1 cup salad with 1 Tbsp low-fat dressing	1 Vegetable 1 Fat	1 cup salad with 1 Tbsp low-fat dressing	1 Vegetable 1 Fat
		1 whole-wheat roll with 1 tsp Smart Balance Buttery Spread	1 Grain 1 Fat	1 whole-wheat roll with 1 tsp Smart Balance Buttery Spread	1 Grain 1 Fat	1 whole-wheat roll with 1 tsp Smart Balance Buttery Spread	1 Grain 1 Fat
Banana Bread (page 34)	1.1 Grain 0.5 Fruit 0.2 Fat	Banana Bread (page 34)	1.1 Grain 0.5 Fruit 0.2 Fat	Banana Bread (page 34)	1.1 Grain 0.5 Fruit 0.2 Fat	Banana Bread (page 34)	1.1 Grain 0.5 Fruit 0.2 Fat
4 ounces nonfat milk	0.5 Milk	4 ounces nonfat milk	0.5 Milk	8 ounces nonfat milk	1 Milk	8 ounces nonfat milk	1 Milk
Food group totals	4.6 Grain 4.4 Protein 2.45 Milk 1.5 Fruit 4.4 Vegetable 3.6 Fat		6 Grain 4.9 Protein 2.5 Milk 1.5 Fruit 4.4 Vegetable 4.8 Fat		7.4 Grain 5.4 Protein 3.3 Milk 2.5 Fruit 4.4 Vegetable 4.9 Fat		8.4 Grain 5.4 Protein 3.3 Milk 2.5 Fruit 4.4 Vegetable 4.9 Fat

Day 5	1,200 Calories Foods	Food group servings	1,500 Calories Foods	Food group servings	1,800 Calories Foods	Food group servings	2,200 Calories Foods	Food group servings
Breakfast	¾ cup Cheerios	1 Grain	1 cup Cheerios	1.25 Grain	1½ cups Cheerios	2 Grain	2¼ cups Cheerios	3 Grain
	4 ounces nonfat milk	0.5 Milk	8 ounces nonfat milk	1 Milk	8 ounces nonfat milk	1 Milk	8 ounces nonfat milk	1 Milk
Snack	1 small banana	1 Fruit	1 small banana	1 Fruit	1 small banana	1 Fruit	1 small banana	1 Fruit
					8 ounces nonfat yogurt	1 Milk	8 ounces nonfat yogurt	1 Milk
Lunch	Chicken Tomato Wrap Sandwich (page 51)	1 Grain 0.25 Vegetable 4 Protein 3.4 Fat	Chicken Tomato Wrap Sandwich (page 51)	1 Grain 0.25 Vegetable 4 Protein 3.4 Fat	Chicken Tomato Wrap Sandwich (page 51)	1 Grain 0.25 Vegetable 4 Protein 3.4 Fat	Chicken Tomato Wrap Sandwich (page 51)	1 Grain 0.25 Vegetable 4 Protein 3.4 Fat
	1 cup raw veggies	1 Vegetable	1 cup raw veggies with 1 Tbsp low-fat dressing	1 Vegetable 1 Fat	1 cup raw veggies with 1 Tbsp low-fat dressing	1 Vegetable 1 Fat	1 cup raw veggies with 1 Tbsp low-fat dressing	1 Vegetable 1 Fat
					12 pretzels	1 Grain	12 pretzels	1 Grain
Snack	Banana Bread (page 34)	1.1 Grain 0.5 Fruit 0.2 Fat	Banana Bread (page 34)	1.1 Grain 0.5 Fruit 0.2 Fat	Banana Bread (page 34)	1.1 Grain 0.5 Fruit 0.2 Fat	Banana Bread (page 34)	1.1 Grain 0.5 Fruit 0.2 Fat
	4 ounces nonfat milk	0.5 Milk	4 ounces nonfat milk	0.5 Milk	8 ounces nonfat milk	1 Milk	8 ounces nonfat milk	1 Milk

Dinner	Plan 1	Plan 2	Plan 3	Plan 4
	Baked potato (6 ounces) with 1 Tbsp low-fat sour cream — 2 Grain, 1 Fat	Baked potato (6 ounces) with 1 Tbsp low-fat sour cream — 2 Grain, 1 Fat	Baked potato (6 ounces) with 1 Tbsp low-fat sour cream — 2 Grain, 1 Fat	Baked potato (6 ounces) with 2 Tbsp low-fat sour cream — 2 Grain, 2 Fat
	1/2 cup cooked broccoli — 1 Vegetable	1/2 cup cooked broccoli — 1 Vegetable	1/2 cup cooked broccoli — 1 Vegetable	1/2 cup cooked broccoli — 1 Vegetable
	1/2 cup watermelon — 0.5 Fruit	1/2 cup watermelon — 0.5 Fruit	1/2 cup watermelon — 0.5 Fruit	1/2 cup watermelon — 0.5 Fruit
	8 ounces nonfat milk — 1 Milk	8 ounces nonfat milk — 1 Milk	8 ounces nonfat milk — 1 Milk	8 ounces nonfat milk — 1 Milk
	1 cup salad — 1 Vegetable	1 cup salad — 1 Vegetable	1 cup salad with 1 Tbsp low-fat dressing and 1 ounce turkey bacon — 1 Vegetable, 1 Fat, 1 Protein	1 cup salad with 1 Tbsp low-fat dressing and 1 ounce turkey bacon — 1 Vegetable, 1 Fat, 1 Protein
	1/4 cup low-fat cottage cheese with 1/2 cup pineapple — 1 Protein, 0.5 Fruit	1/4 cup low-fat cottage cheese with 1/2 cup pineapple — 1 Protein, 0.5 Fruit	1/4 cup low-fat cottage cheese with 1/2 cup pineapple — 1 Protein, 0.5 Fruit	1/4 cup low-fat cottage cheese with 1/2 cup pineapple — 1 Protein, 0.5 Fruit
Food group totals	5.1 Grain, 5 Protein, 2 Milk, 2.5 Fruit, 3.25 Vegetable, 4.6 Fat	5.26 Grain, 5 Protein, 2.5 Milk, 2.5 Fruit, 3.25 Vegetable, 5.6 Fat	7.1 Grain, 6 Protein, 4 Milk, 2.5 Fruit, 3.25 Vegetable, 6.6 Fat	8.1 Grain, 6 Protein, 4 Milk, 2.5 Fruit, 3.25 Vegetable, 7.6 Fat

WEEK 2	1,200 Calories		1,500 Calories		1,800 Calories		2,200 Calories	
Day 6	Foods	Food group servings	Foods	Food group servings	Foods	Food group servings	Foods	Food group servings
Breakfast	French Toast (page 29)	2 Grain 0.1 Milk 1 Protein 1.2 Fat	French Toast (page 29)	2 Grain 0.1 Milk 1 Protein 1.2 Fat	1½ servings French Toast (page 29)	3 Grain 0.15 Milk 1.5 Protein 1.8 Fat	1½ servings French Toast (page 29)	3 Grain 0.15 Milk 1.5 Protein 1.8 Fat
	8 ounces nonfat milk	1 Milk	8 ounces nonfat milk	1 Milk	12 ounces nonfat milk	1.5 Milk	12 ounces nonfat milk	1.5 Milk
Snack	1 orange	1 Fruit	1 orange	1 Fruit	1 orange	1 Fruit	1 orange	1 Fruit
Lunch	Spinach salad: 2 cups spinach, 1 ounce turkey bacon, ½ cup mushrooms, 1 Tbsp low-fat dressing	3 Vegetable 1 Protein 1 Fat	Spinach salad: 2 cups spinach, 1 ounce turkey bacon, ½ hard-boiled egg, ¼ cup dried cranberries, ½ cup mushrooms, 1 Tbsp low-fat dressing	3 Vegetable 1 Fruit 1.5 Protein 1 Fat	Spinach salad: 2 cups spinach, 1 ounce turkey bacon, ½ hard-boiled egg, ¼ cup dried cranberries, ½ cup mushrooms, 1 Tbsp low-fat dressing	3 Vegetable 1 Fruit 1.5 Protein 1 Fat	Spinach salad: 2 cups spinach, 1 ounce turkey bacon, ½ hard-boiled egg, ¼ cup dried cranberries, ½ cup mushrooms, 1 Tbsp low-fat dressing	3 Vegetable 1 Fruit 1.5 Protein 1 Fat
Snack	4 rye crisps	1 Grain	8 rye crisps	2 Grain	8 rye crisps	2 Grain	8 rye crisps	2 Grain
	Fresh Fruit Dip (page 66)	1 Fruit 2 Fat	Fresh Fruit Dip (page 66)	1 Fruit 2 Fat	Fresh Fruit Dip (page 66)	1 Fruit 2 Fat	Fresh Fruit Dip (page 66)	1 Fruit 2 Fat
Dinner	Chicken with Dijon and Apricot Sauce (page 90)	0.25 Milk 3.4 Protein 1.4 Fat	Chicken with Dijon and Apricot Sauce (page 90)	0.25 Milk 3.4 Protein 1.4 Fat	Chicken with Dijon and Apricot Sauce (page 90)	0.25 Milk 3.4 Protein 1.4 Fat	Chicken with Dijon and Apricot Sauce (page 90)	0.25 Milk 3.4 Protein 1.4 Fat

Food / Amount	Equivalents	Food / Amount	Equivalents	Food / Amount	Equivalents	Food / Amount	Equivalents
1/2 cup couscous	1 Grain	1/2 cup couscous	1 Grain	1/2 cup couscous	1 Grain	1/2 cup couscous	1 Grain
1 cup steamed broccoli	1 Vegetable	1 cup steamed broccoli	1 Vegetable	1 cup steamed broccoli	1 Vegetable	1 cup steamed broccoli	1 Vegetable
Brownie Fruit Pizza (page 178)	0.3 Grain 0.5 Fruit 0.5 Fat	Brownie Fruit Pizza (page 178)	0.3 Grain 0.5 Fruit 0.5 Fat	Brownie Fruit Pizza (page 178)	0.3 Grain 0.5 Fruit 0.5 Fat	Brownie Fruit Pizza (page 178)	0.3 Grain 0.5 Fruit 0.5 Fat
8 ounces nonfat milk	1 Milk	8 ounces nonfat milk	1 Milk	12 ounces nonfat milk	1.5 Milk	12 ounces nonfat milk	1.5 Milk
Food group totals	4.3 Grain 5.4 Protein 2.35 Milk 2.5 Fruit 4 Vegetable 6.1 Fat	Food group totals	5.3 Grain 5.9 Protein 2.25 Milk 3.5 Fruit 4 Vegetable 6.1 Fat	Food group totals	6.3 Grain 6.9 Protein 3.4 Milk 3.5 Fruit 4 Vegetable 6.7 Fat	Food group totals	6.3 Grain 6.4 Protein 3.4 Milk 3.5 Fruit 4 Vegetable 6.7 Fat

Day 7	1,200 Calories Foods	Food group servings	1,500 Calories Foods	Food group servings	1,800 Calories Foods	Food group servings	2,200 Calories Foods	Food group servings
Breakfast	1 whole-wheat Eggo frozen waffle with 1 Tbsp reduced-calorie syrup	1 Grain	1 whole-wheat Eggo frozen waffle with 1 Tbsp reduced-calorie syrup	1 Grain	1 whole-wheat Eggo frozen waffle with 1 Tbsp reduced-calorie syrup	1 Grain	1 whole-wheat Eggo frozen waffle with 1 Tbsp reduced-calorie syrup	1 Grain
	½ cup strawberries	0.5 Fruit	½ cup strawberries	0.5 Fruit	½ cup strawberries	0.5 Fruit	½ cup strawberries	0.5 Fruit
	8 ounces nonfat milk	1 Milk	8 ounces nonfat milk	1 Milk	8 ounces nonfat milk	1 Milk	8 ounces nonfat milk	1 Milk
Snack	12 grapes	1 Fruit	12 grapes	1 Fruit	12 grapes	1 Fruit	12 grapes	1 Fruit
					1 ounce low-fat string cheese	1 Protein	1 ounce low-fat string cheese	1 Protein
Lunch	Ham and Cheese Turnover (page 48)	1 Grain 0.1 Vegetable 0.13 Milk 1.4 Protein 1.2 Fat	Ham and Cheese Turnover (page 48)	1 Grain 0.1 Vegetable 0.13 Milk 1.4 Protein 1.2 Fat	Ham and Cheese Turnover (page 48)	1 Grain 0.1 Vegetable 0.13 Milk 1.4 Protein 1.2 Fat	Ham and Cheese Turnover (page 48)	1 Grain 0.1 Vegetable 0.13 Milk 1.4 Protein 1.2 Fat
	1 cup edamame	1 Vegetable	1½ cups edamame	1.5 Vegetable	1½ cups edamame	1.5 Vegetable	1½ cups edamame	1.5 Vegetable
					8 ounces nonfat yogurt with ¼ cup mixed nuts	1 Milk 1 Protein 1 Fat	8 ounces nonfat yogurt with ¼ cup mixed nuts	1 Milk 1 Protein 1 Fat

	Plan 1	Plan 2	Plan 3	Plan 4
Snack	1 Chocolate Chip Cookie (page 173) — 0.5 Grain, 1 Fat	1 Chocolate Chip Cookie (page 173) — 0.5 Grain, 1 Fat	1 Chocolate Chip Cookie (page 173) — 0.5 Grain, 1 Fat	2 Chocolate Chip Cookies (page 173) — 1 Grain, 2 Fat
	8 ounces nonfat milk — 1 Milk	8 ounces nonfat milk — 1 Milk	8 ounces nonfat milk — 1 Milk	8 ounces nonfat milk — 1 Milk
Dinner	Turkey Chimichangas (page 85) — 1 Grain, 0.7 Vegetable, 0.8 Protein, 2 Fat	Turkey Chimichangas (page 85) — 1 Grain, 0.7 Vegetable, 0.8 Protein, 2 Fat	2 servings Turkey Chimichangas (page 85) — 2 Grain, 1.4 Vegetable, 1.6 Protein, 4 Fat	2 servings Turkey Chimichangas (page 85) — 2 Grain, 1.4 Vegetable, 1.6 Protein, 4 Fat
	1 cup salad with 1 Tbsp low-fat dressing — 1 Vegetable, 1 Fat	1 cup salad with 1 Tbsp low-fat dressing — 1 Vegetable, 1 Fat	1 cup salad with 1 Tbsp low-fat dressing — 1 Vegetable, 1 Fat	1 cup salad with 1 Tbsp low-fat dressing — 1 Vegetable, 1 Fat
	1 cup mixed fruit with 1 Tbsp nonfat nondairy topping — 1 Fruit	1 cup mixed fruit with 1 Tbsp nonfat nondairy topping — 1 Fruit	1 cup mixed fruit with 1 Tbsp nonfat nondairy topping — 1 Fruit	1 cup mixed fruit with 1 Tbsp nonfat nondairy topping — 1 Fruit
Food group totals	3.5 Grain, 2.2 Protein, 2.13 Milk, 2.5 Fruit, 2.8 Vegetable, 5.2 Fat	3.5 Grain, 2.2 Protein, 2.13 Milk, 2.5 Fruit, 3.3 Vegetable, 5.2 Fat	4.5 Grain, 5 Protein, 3.13 Milk, 2.5 Fruit, 4 Vegetable, 8.2 Fat	5 Grain, 5 Protein, 3.13 Milk, 2.5 Fruit, 4 Vegetable, 9.2 Fat

WEEK 3	1,200 Calories		1,500 Calories		1,800 Calories		2,200 Calories	
Day 1	Foods	Food group servings	Foods	Food group servings	Foods	Food group servings	Foods	Food group servings
Breakfast	¾ cup Cheerios	1 Grain	¾ cup Cheerios	1 Grain	1½ cups Cheerios	2 Grain	1½ cups Cheerios	2 Grain
	4 ounces nonfat milk	0.5 Milk	4 ounces nonfat milk	0.5 Milk	6 ounces nonfat milk	0.75 Milk	6 ounces nonfat milk	0.75 Milk
Snack	¼ cup raisins	1 Fruit	¼ cup raisins	1 Fruit	½ cup raisins	2 Fruit	½ cup raisins	2 Fruit
Lunch	Peanut-butter sandwich: 2 slices whole-wheat bread, 1 Tbsp natural peanut butter, 1 Tbsp all-fruit jelly	2 Grain 0.5 Protein 1 Fat	Peanut-butter sandwich: 2 slices whole-wheat bread, 1 Tbsp natural peanut butter, 1 Tbsp all-fruit jelly	2 Grain 0.5 Protein 1 Fat	Peanut-butter sandwich: 2 slices whole-wheat bread, 1 Tbsp natural peanut butter, 1 Tbsp all-fruit jelly	2 Grain 0.5 Protein 1 Fat	Peanut-butter sandwich: 2 slices whole-wheat bread, 1 Tbsp natural peanut butter, 1 Tbsp all-fruit jelly	2 Grain 0.5 Protein 1 Fat
	8 ounces nonfat milk	1 Milk	8 ounces nonfat milk	1 Milk	8 ounces nonfat milk	1 Milk	8 ounces nonfat milk	1 Milk
	1 cup carrots	1 Vegetable	1 cup carrots	1 Vegetable	1 cup carrots	1 Vegetable	1 cup carrots	1 Vegetable
					½ cup sliced cucumber with 1 Tbsp low-fat ranch dressing	0.5 Vegetable 1 Fat	½ cup sliced cucumber with 1 Tbsp low-fat ranch dressing	0.5 Vegetable 1 Fat
Snack	1 orange	1 Fruit	1 orange	1 Fruit	1 orange	1 Fruit	1 orange	1 Fruit
Dinner	Barbecued Chicken (page 87)	3 Protein 0.6 Fat	Barbecued Chicken (page 87)	3 Protein 0.6 Fat	Barbecued Chicken (page 87)	3 Protein 0.6 Fat	1½ servings Barbecued Chicken (page 87)	4.5 Protein 0.9 Fat

	Meal Plan 1		Meal Plan 2		Meal Plan 3		Meal Plan 4	
	Broccoli Salad (page 146)	0.5 Vegetable 0.5 Protein 1 Fat	Broccoli Salad (page 146)	0.5 Vegetable 0.5 Protein 1 Fat	Broccoli Salad (page 146)	0.5 Vegetable 0.5 Protein 1 Fat	Broccoli Salad (page 146)	0.5 Vegetable 0.5 Protein 1 Fat
	Baked Onion Rings (page 61)	0.7 Grain 0.6 Vegetable 0.2 Fat	Baked Onion Rings (page 61)	0.7 Grain 0.6 Vegetable 0.2 Fat	Baked Onion Rings (page 61)	0.7 Grain 0.6 Vegetable 0.2 Fat	Baked Onion Rings (page 61)	0.7 Grain 0.6 Vegetable 0.2 Fat
	4 ounces nonfat milk	0.5 Milk	6 ounces nonfat milk	0.75 Milk	6 ounces nonfat milk	0.75 Milk	6 ounces nonfat milk	0.75 Milk
			1 whole-wheat roll	1 Grain	1 whole-wheat roll	1 Grain	1 whole-wheat roll	1 Grain
	Fruit and Yogurt Parfait (page 65)	1 Grain 0.5 Fruit 0.5 Milk 0.4 Fat	Fruit and Yogurt Parfait (page 65)	1 Grain 0.5 Fruit 0.5 Milk 0.4 Fat	Fruit and Yogurt Parfait (page 65)	1 Grain 0.5 Fruit 0.5 Milk 0.4 Fat	Fruit and Yogurt Parfait (page 65)	1 Grain 0.5 Fruit 0.5 Milk 0.4 Fat
Food group totals		4.7 Grain 4 Protein 2.5 Milk 2.5 Fruit 2.1 Vegetable 2.8 Fat		6.4 Grain 4 Protein 2.75 Milk 2.5 Fruit 2.1 Vegetable 2.8 Fat		8.7 Grain 4 Protein 3 Milk 3.5 Fruit 3.6 Vegetable 3.8 Fat		6.7 Grain 5.5 Protein 3 Milk 3.5 Fruit 7.1 Vegetable 4.1 Fat

WEEK 3

Day 2	1,200 Calories Foods	Food group servings	1,500 Calories Foods	Food group servings	1,800 Calories Foods	Food group servings	2,200 Calories Foods	Food group servings
Breakfast	½ whole-wheat bagel with 1 Tbsp low-fat cream cheese and 1 slice tomato	1 Grain 0.2 Vegetable 1 Fat	1 whole-wheat bagel with 1 Tbsp low-fat cream cheese and 1 slice tomato	2 Grain 0.2 Vegetable 1 Fat	1 whole-wheat bagel with 1 Tbsp low-fat cream cheese and 1 slice tomato	2 Grain 0.2 Vegetable 1 Fat	1 whole-wheat bagel with 1 Tbsp low-fat cream cheese and 1 slice tomato	2 Grain 0.2 Vegetable 1 Fat
	12 grapes	1 Fruit	18 grapes	1.5 Fruit	24 grapes	2 Fruit	24 grapes	2 Fruit
Snack	Purple Moo (page 72)	1 Fruit 0.75 Milk 0.2 Fat	Purple Moo (page 72)	1 Fruit 0.75 Milk 0.2 Fat	Purple Moo (page 72)	1 Fruit 0.75 Milk 0.2 Fat	Purple Moo (page 72)	1 Fruit 0.75 Milk 0.2 Fat
Lunch	Egg salad sandwich: 2 slices whole-wheat bread, 1 hard-boiled egg, 1 Tbsp low-fat mayonnaise, ½ Tbsp pickle relish	2 Grain 1 Protein 1 Fat	Egg salad sandwich: 2 slices whole-wheat bread, 1 hard-boiled egg, 1 Tbsp low-fat mayonnaise, ½ Tbsp pickle relish	2 Grain 1 Protein 1 Fat	1½ egg salad sandwiches: 3 slices whole-wheat bread, 2 hard-boiled eggs, 1 Tbsp low-fat mayonnaise, ½ Tbsp pickle relish	3 Grain 2 Protein 1 Fat	1½ egg salad sandwiches: 3 slices whole-wheat bread, 2 hard-boiled eggs, 1 Tbsp low-fat mayonnaise, ½ Tbsp pickle relish	3 Grain 2 Protein 1 Fat
Snack	Onion Dip (page 67) with 1 cup of carrots and celery	0.6 Milk 0.2 Fruit 1 Vegetable	Onion Dip (page 67) with 1 cup of carrots and celery	0.6 Milk 0.2 Fruit 1 Vegetable	Onion Dip (page 67) with 1 cup of carrots and celery	0.6 Milk 0.2 Fruit 1 Vegetable	Onion Dip (page 67) with 1 cup of carrots and celery	0.6 Milk 0.2 Fruit 1 Vegetable
Dinner	Tropical Shrimp Skewers (page 102)	0.5 Fruit 3.4 Protein 0.4 Fat	Tropical Shrimp Skewers (page 102)	0.5 Fruit 3.4 Protein 0.4 Fat	Tropical Shrimp Skewers (page 102)	0.5 Fruit 3.4 Protein 0.4 Fat	Tropical Shrimp Skewers (page 102)	0.5 Fruit 3.4 Protein 0.4 Fat

	1 Grain	1 Grain	2 Grain	2 Grain 1 Fat
	½ cup brown rice	½ cup brown rice	1 cup brown rice	1 cup brown rice with 1 tsp Smart Balance Buttery Spread
	1 Vegetable	1 Vegetable	1 Vegetable	1 Vegetable
	½ cup cooked squash	½ cup cooked squash	½ cup cooked squash	½ cup cooked squash
			1 Milk	1 Milk
			8 ounces nonfat milk	8 ounces nonfat milk
Food group totals	4 Grain 4.4 Protein 1.35 Milk 2.7 Fruit 2.2 Vegetable 2.6 Fat	5 Grain 4.4 Protein 1.35 Milk 3.2 Fruit 2.2 Vegetable 2.6 Fat	7 Grain 5.4 Protein 2.35 Milk 3.7 Fruit 2.2 Vegetable 2.6 Fat	7 Grain 5.4 Protein 2.35 Milk 3.7 Fruit 2.2 Vegetable 3.6 Fat

WEEK 3

Day 3	1,200 Calories		1,500 Calories		1,800 Calories		2,200 Calories	
	Foods	Food group servings	Foods	Food group servings	Foods	Food group servings	Foods	Food group servings
Breakfast	8 ounces nonfat yogurt	1 Milk	8 ounces nonfat yogurt	1 Milk	8 ounces nonfat yogurt	1 Milk	8 ounces nonfat yogurt with ¼ cup nuts	1 Milk, 1 Protein, 1 Fat
	½ small banana	0.5 Fruit	½ small banana	0.5 Fruit	½ small banana	0.5 Fruit	½ small banana	0.5 Fruit
	1 slice whole-wheat toast with 1 Tbsp reduced-calorie all-fruit jelly	1 Grain	1 slice whole-wheat toast with 1 Tbsp reduced-calorie all-fruit jelly	1 Grain	2 slices whole-wheat toast with 1 Tbsp reduced-calorie all-fruit jelly	2 Grain	2 slices whole-wheat toast with 1 Tbsp reduced-calorie all-fruit jelly	2 Grain
Snack	2 plums	1 Fruit	2 plums	1 Fruit	2 plums	1 Fruit	2 plums	1 Fruit
Lunch	2 ounces lean turkey in 1 small whole-wheat pita with mustard, lettuce, tomato, 1 Tbsp low-fat mayonnaise	2 Protein, 1 Grain, 1 Fat	2 ounces lean turkey in 1 small whole-wheat pita with mustard, lettuce, tomato, 1 Tbsp low-fat mayonnaise	2 Protein, 1 Grain, 1 Fat	2 ounces lean turkey in 1 small whole-wheat pita with mustard, lettuce, tomato, 1 Tbsp low-fat mayonnaise	2 Protein, 1 Grain, 1 Fat	2 ounces lean turkey in 1 small whole-wheat pita with mustard, lettuce, tomato, 1 Tbsp low-fat mayonnaise	2 Protein, 1 Grain, 1 Fat
	1 ounce low-fat string cheese	1 Protein	1 ounce low-fat string cheese	1 Protein	1 ounce low-fat string cheese	1 Protein	1 ounce low-fat string cheese	1 Protein
	4 ounces tomato juice	1 Vegetable	6 ounces tomato juice	1.5 Vegetable	6 ounces tomato juice	1.5 Vegetable	6 ounces tomato juice	1.5 Vegetable
Snack	½ serving Baked Potato Skins (page 63)	1 Grain, 0.5 Protein, 0.4 Fat	½ serving Baked Potato Skins (page 63)	1 Grain, 0.5 Protein, 0.4 Fat	1½ servings Baked Potato Skins (page 63)	3 Grain, 1.5 Protein, 1.6 Fat	1½ servings Baked Potato Skins (page 63)	3 Grain, 1.5 Protein, 1.6 Fat

	Plan 1	Plan 2	Plan 3	Plan 4
Dinner	Caribbean Pasta Salad (page 122) 1 Grain 1 Vegetable 0.2 Milk 0.4 Protein 1.4 Fat	Caribbean Pasta Salad (page 122) 1 Grain 1 Vegetable 0.2 Milk 0.4 Protein 1.4 Fat	1½ servings Caribbean Pasta Salad (page 122) 1.5 Grain 1.5 Vegetable 0.3 Milk 0.6 Protein 2.1 Fat	1½ servings Caribbean Pasta Salad (page 122) 1.5 Grain 1.5 Vegetable 0.3 Milk 0.6 Protein 2.1 Fat
	8 ounces nonfat milk 1 Milk	8 ounces nonfat milk 1 Milk	8 ounces nonfat milk 1 Milk	8 ounces nonfat milk 1 Milk
	Baked Apples à la Mode (page 187) 0.8 Fruit 0.2 Milk 0.3 Fat	Baked Apples à la Mode (page 187) 0.8 Fruit 0.2 Milk 0.3 Fat	Baked Apples à la Mode (page 187) 0.8 Fruit 0.2 Milk 0.3 Fat	Baked Apples à la Mode (page 187) 0.8 Fruit 0.2 Milk 0.3 Fat
Food group totals	4 Grain 3.9 Protein 2.4 Milk 2.3 Fruit 2 Vegetable 3.1 Fat	4 Grain 3.9 Protein 2.4 Milk 2.3 Fruit 2.5 Vegetable 3.1 Fat	7.5 Grain 5.1 Protein 2.5 Milk 2.3 Fruit 3 Vegetable 5 Fat	7.5 Grain 6.1 Protein 2.5 Milk 2.3 Fruit 3 Vegetable 6 Fat

Day 4	1,200 Calories		1,500 Calories		1,800 Calories		2,200 Calories	
	Foods	Food group servings	Foods	Food group servings	Foods	Food group servings	Foods	Food group servings
Breakfast	½ cup oatmeal	1 Grain	½ cup oatmeal	1 Grain	½ cup oatmeal	1 Grain	1 cup oatmeal	2 Grain
	4 ounces nonfat milk	0.5 Milk	4 ounces nonfat milk	0.5 Milk	4 ounces nonfat milk	0.5 Milk	4 ounces nonfat milk	0.5 Milk
Snack	½ small banana	0.5 Fruit	½ small banana	0.5 Fruit	1 small banana	1 Fruit	1 small banana	1 Fruit
			2 mini bagels	1 Grain	4 mini bagels with 2 tsp Smart Balance Buttery Spread	2 Grain 2 Fat	4 mini bagels with 2 tsp Smart Balance Buttery Spread	2 Grain 2 Fat
Lunch	Chicken Pita Pockets (page 50)	1 Grain 2 Protein 0.2 Vegetable 1.4 Fat	Chicken Pita Pockets (page 50)	1 Grain 2 Protein 0.2 Vegetable 1.4 Fat	Chicken Pita Pockets (page 50)	1 Grain 2 Protein 0.2 Vegetable 1.4 Fat	Chicken Pita Pockets (page 50)	1 Grain 2 Protein 0.2 Vegetable 1.4 Fat
	1 cup salad with 1 Tbsp low-fat dressing	1 Vegetable 1 Fat	1 cup salad with 1 Tbsp low-fat dressing	1 Vegetable 1 Fat	1 cup salad with 1 Tbsp low-fat dressing	1 Vegetable 1 Fat	1 cup salad with 1 Tbsp low-fat dressing	1 Vegetable 1 Fat
	4 ounces nonfat yogurt	0.5 Milk	4 ounces nonfat yogurt	0.5 Milk	8 ounces nonfat yogurt with ¼ cup trail mix	1 Milk 1 Protein 2 Fat	8 ounces nonfat yogurt with ¼ cup trail mix	1 Milk 1 Protein 2 Fat
Snack	Waldorf Salad (page 58)	0.2 Vegetable 2 Fruit 0.2 Fat	Waldorf Salad (page 58)	0.2 Vegetable 2 Fruit 0.2 Fat	Waldorf Salad (page 58)	0.2 Vegetable 2 Fruit 0.2 Fat	Waldorf Salad (page 58)	0.2 Vegetable 2 Fruit 0.2 Fat

Dinner				
Quick Sloppy Joe Casserole (page 114)	Quick Sloppy Joe Casserole (page 114)	1½ servings Quick Sloppy Joe Casserole (page 114)	1½ servings Quick Sloppy Joe Casserole (page 114)
0.5 Grain 2 Protein 0.6 Fat	0.5 Grain 2 Protein 0.6 Fat	0.75 Grain 3 Protein 0.9 Fat	0.75 Grain 3 Protein 0.9 Fat
1 cup steamed broccoli	1 cup steamed broccoli	1½ cups steamed broccoli	1½ cups steamed broccoli
1 Vegetable	1 Vegetable	1.5 Vegetable	1.5 Vegetable
4 ounces nonfat milk	4 ounces nonfat milk	8 ounces nonfat milk	8 ounces nonfat milk
0.5 Milk	0.5 Milk	1 Milk	1 Milk
½ serving Crispy French Fries (page 158)	½ serving Crispy French Fries (page 158)	Crispy French Fries (page 158)	Crispy French Fries (page 158)
1.5 Grain 0.25 Protein	1.5 Grain 0.25 Protein	2.9 Grain 0.5 Protein	2.9 Grain 0.5 Protein
Chocolate Pudding (page 188)	Chocolate Pudding (page 188)	Chocolate Pudding (page 188)	Chocolate Pudding (page 188)
0.3 Milk 0.2 Fat	0.3 Milk 0.2 Fat	0.3 Milk 0.2 Fat	0.3 Milk 0.2 Fat

Food group totals			
4 Grain 2.25 Protein 1.8 Milk 2.5 Fruit 2.4 Vegetable 3.4 Fat	5 Grain 4.25 Protein 1.8 Milk 2.5 Fruit 2.4 Vegetable 3.4 Fat	6.65 Grain 6.5 Protein 2.8 Milk 3 Fruit 2.9 Vegetable 7.7 Fat	8.65 Grain 6.5 Protein 3.8 Milk 3 Fruit 2.9 Vegetable 7.7 Fat

Day 5	1,200 Calories Foods	Food group servings	1,500 Calories Foods	Food group servings	1,800 Calories Foods	Food group servings	2,200 Calories Foods	Food group servings
Breakfast	Strawberry Licuado (page 73)	1 Fruit 0.5 Milk 0.2 Fat	Strawberry Licuado (page 73)	1 Fruit 0.5 Milk 0.2 Fat	Strawberry Licuado (page 73)	1 Fruit 0.5 Milk 0.2 Fat	Strawberry Licuado (page 73)	1 Fruit 0.5 Milk 0.2 Fat
	½ English muffin with 1 Tbsp reduced-calorie all-fruit jelly	1 Grain	½ English muffin with 1 Tbsp reduced-calorie all-fruit jelly	1 Grain	2 English muffins with 1 Tbsp reduced-calorie all-fruit jelly	4 Grain	2 English muffins with 1 Tbsp reduced-calorie all-fruit jelly	4 Grain
Snack	½ cup low-fat cottage cheese	1 Protein	½ cup low-fat cottage cheese	1 Protein	½ cup low-fat cottage cheese	1 Protein	½ cup low-fat cottage cheese	1 Protein
Lunch	Roast beef sandwich: 2 slices whole-wheat toast, 1 ounce roast beef, lettuce, tomato, mustard	2 Grain 1 Protein	Roast beef sandwich: 2 slices whole-wheat toast, 1 ounce roast beef, with 1 Tbsp low-fat mayonnaise and lettuce, tomato, mustard	2 Grain 1 Protein 1 Fat	Roast beef sandwich: 2 slices whole-wheat toast, 2 ounces roast beef, with 1 Tbsp low-fat mayonnaise and lettuce, tomato, mustard	2 Grain 2 Protein 1 Fat	Roast beef sandwich: 2 slices whole-wheat toast, 3 ounces roast beef, with 1 Tbsp low-fat mayonnaise and lettuce, tomato, mustard	2 Grain 3 Protein 1 Fat
	1 apple	1 Fruit	1 apple	1 Fruit	1 apple	1 Fruit	1 apple	1 Fruit
	4 ounces nonfat milk	0.5 Milk	4 ounces nonfat milk	0.5 Milk	8 ounces nonfat milk	1 Milk	8 ounces nonfat milk	1 Milk
	1 cup snap peas	1 Vegetable	1 cup snap peas	1 Vegetable	1 cup snap peas	1 Vegetable	1 cup snap peas	1 Vegetable
Snack	3 cups air-popped or microwave-light popcorn	1 Grain	3 cups air-popped or microwave-light popcorn	1 Grain	3 cups air-popped or microwave-light popcorn	1 Grain	3 cups air-popped or microwave-light popcorn	1 Grain

	Plan 1		Plan 2		Plan 3		Plan 4	
Dinner	Chicken Tortilla Soup (page 130)	0.62 Grain 1 Vegetable 2 Protein 1.4 Fat	Chicken Tortilla Soup (page 130)	0.62 Grain 1 Vegetable 2 Protein 1.4 Fat	12 grapes	1 Fruit	12 grapes	1 Fruit
	1 cup salad with 1 Tbsp low-fat dressing	1 Vegetable 1 Fat	1 cup salad with 1 Tbsp low-fat dressing	1 Vegetable 1 Fat	Chicken Tortilla Soup (page 130)	0.62 Grain 1 Vegetable 2 Protein 1.4 Fat	Chicken Tortilla Soup (page 130)	0.62 Grain 1 Vegetable 2 Protein 1.4 Fat
			1 whole-wheat roll	1 Grain	1 cup salad with 1 Tbsp low-fat dressing	1 Vegetable 1 Fat	1 cup salad with 1 Tbsp low-fat dressing	1 Vegetable 1 Fat
					1 whole-wheat roll with 1 tsp Smart Balance Buttery Spread	1 Grain 1 Fat	1 whole-wheat roll with 1 tsp Smart Balance Buttery Spread	1 Grain 1 Fat
	Brownies (page 177)	0.3 Grain 0.3 Milk 1 Fat	Brownies (page 177)	0.3 Grain 0.3 Milk 1 Fat	Brownies (page 177)	0.3 Grain 0.3 Milk 1 Fat	Brownies (page 177)	0.3 Grain 0.3 Milk 1 Fat
	4 ounces nonfat milk	0.5 Milk	4 ounces nonfat milk	0.5 Milk	8 ounces nonfat milk	1 Milk	8 ounces nonfat milk	1 Milk
Food group totals		4.92 Grain 4 Protein 1.8 Milk 2 Fruit 3 Vegetable 3.6 Fat		5.92 Grain 4 Protein 2.3 Milk 2 Fruit 3 Vegetable 4.6 Fat		8.92 Grain 5 Protein 2.3 Milk 3 Fruit 3 Vegetable 5.6 Fat		8.92 Grain 6 Protein 2.8 Milk 3.5 Fruit 3 Vegetable 5.6 Fat

WEEK 3

Day 6	1,200 Calories		1,500 Calories		1,800 Calories		2,200 Calories	
	Foods	Food group servings	Foods	Food group servings	Foods	Food group servings	Foods	Food group servings
Breakfast	Breakfast Pizza (page 30)	2.4 Grain 0.2 Vegetable 1 Protein 2 Fat	Breakfast Pizza (page 30)	2.4 Grain 0.2 Vegetable 1 Protein 2 Fat	Breakfast Pizza (page 30)	2.4 Grain 0.2 Vegetable 1 Protein 2 Fat	Breakfast Pizza (page 30)	2.4 Grain 0.2 Vegetable 1 Protein 2 Fat
	8 ounces nonfat milk	1 Milk	8 ounces nonfat milk	1 Milk	12 ounces nonfat milk	1.5 Milk	12 ounces nonfat milk	1.5 Milk
Snack	1 apple	1 Fruit	1 apple	1 Fruit	1 apple with 1 Tbsp natural peanut butter	1 Fruit 0.5 Protein 1 Fat	1 apple with 1 Tbsp natural peanut butter	1 Fruit 0.5 Protein 1 Fat
Lunch	Chicken Tortilla Soup (page 130)	0.62 Grain 1 Vegetable 2 Protein 1.4 Fat	Chicken Tortilla Soup (page 130)	0.62 Grain 1 Vegetable 2 Protein 1.4 Fat	Chicken Tortilla Soup (page 130)	0.62 Grain 1 Vegetable 2 Protein 1.4 Fat	Chicken Tortilla Soup (page 130)	0.62 Grain 1 Vegetable 2 Protein 1.4 Fat
			1 small banana	1 Fruit	1 small banana	1 Fruit	1 small banana	1 Fruit
					1 whole-wheat bagel	1 Grain	1 whole-wheat bagel	1 Grain
Snack	½ serving Hot Artichoke Dip (page 67) with 1 cup raw vegetables	1.25 Vegetable 0.1 Protein 1.1 Fat	Hot Artichoke Dip (page 67) with 1 cup raw vegetables	1.5 Vegetable 0.2 Protein 2.2 Fat	Hot Artichoke Dip (page 67) with 1 cup raw vegetables	1.5 Vegetable 0.2 Protein 2.2 Fat	Hot Artichoke Dip (page 67) with 1 cup raw vegetables	1.5 Vegetable 0.2 Protein 2.2 Fat

Meal	Item	Food groups	Item	Food groups	Item	Food groups	Item	Food groups
Dinner			6 low-fat wheat crackers	1 Grain	6 low-fat wheat crackers	1 Grain	6 low-fat wheat crackers	1 Grain
	Pineapple Beef (page 77)	0.5 Vegetable, 0.25 Fruit, 2.7 Protein, 1 Fat	Pineapple Beef (page 77)	0.5 Vegetable, 0.25 Fruit, 2.7 Protein, 1 Fat	Pineapple Beef (page 77)	0.5 Vegetable, 0.25 Fruit, 2.7 Protein, 1 Fat	Pineapple Beef (page 77)	0.5 Vegetable, 0.25 Fruit, 2.7 Protein, 1 Fat
	1 cup fruit	1 Fruit	1 cup fruit	1 Fruit	1 cup fruit	1 Fruit	1 cup fruit	1 Fruit
	8 ounces nonfat milk	1 Milk	8 ounces nonfat milk	1 Milk	12 ounces nonfat milk	1.5 Milk	12 ounces nonfat milk	1.5 Milk
	2 Oatmeal Raisin Cookies (page 175)	1 Grain, 0.2 Fruit, 0.6 Fat	2 Oatmeal Raisin Cookies (page 175)	1 Grain, 0.2 Fruit, 0.6 Fat	4 Oatmeal Raisin Cookies (page 175)	2 Grain, 0.4 Fruit, 1.2 Fat	4 Oatmeal Raisin Cookies (page 175)	2 Grain, 0.4 Fruit, 1.2 Fat
Food group totals		4.02 Grain, 5.8 Protein, 2 Milk, 2.45 Fruit, 2.3 Vegetable, 6.1 Fat		5.02 Grain, 5.9 Protein, 2 Milk, 3.45 Fruit, 3.2 Vegetable, 7.2 Fat		7.02 Grain, 6.4 Protein, 3 Milk, 3.65 Fruit, 3.2 Vegetable, 8.8 Fat		7.02 Grain, 6.4 Protein, 3 Milk, 3.65 Fruit, 3.2 Vegetable, 8.8 Fat

Day 7	1,200 Calories		1,500 Calories		1,800 Calories		2,200 Calories	
	Foods	Food group servings	Foods	Food group servings	Foods	Food group servings	Foods	Food group servings
Breakfast	2 Pumpkin Pancakes (page 31)	1.5 Grain 0.2 Milk 0.1 Protein 0.4 Fat	2 Pumpkin Pancakes (page 31)	1.5 Grain 0.2 Milk 0.1 Protein 0.4 Fat	2 Pumpkin Pancakes (page 31)	1.5 Grain 0.2 Milk 0.1 Protein 0.4 Fat	4 Pumpkin Pancakes (page 31)	3 Grain 0.4 Milk 0.2 Protein 0.8 Fat
	4 ounces nonfat milk	0.5 Milk	4 ounces nonfat milk	0.5 Milk	8 ounces nonfat milk	1 Milk	8 ounces nonfat milk	1 Milk
Snack	½ cup strawberries	0.5 Fruit	1 cup strawberries	1 Fruit	1 cup strawberries	1 Fruit	1 cup strawberries	1 Fruit
	4 ounces nonfat yogurt	0.5 Milk	4 ounces nonfat yogurt	0.5 Milk	8 ounces nonfat yogurt	1 Milk	8 ounces nonfat yogurt	1 Milk
Lunch	Cut-Out Tuna Sandwich Shapes (page 43)	2 Grain 0.5 Vegetable 3 Protein 1.4 Fat	Cut-Out Tuna Sandwich Shapes (page 43)	2 Grain 0.5 Vegetable 3 Protein 1.4 Fat	Cut-Out Tuna Sandwich Shapes (page 43)	2 Grain 0.5 Vegetable 3 Protein 1.4 Fat	Cut-Out Tuna Sandwich Shapes (page 43)	2 Grain 0.5 Vegetable 3 Protein 1.4 Fat
	1 cup salad with 1 Tbsp low-fat dressing	1 Vegetable 1 Fat	1 cup salad with 1 Tbsp low-fat dressing and ⅛ avocado	1 Vegetable 2 Fat	1 cup salad with 1 Tbsp low-fat dressing and ⅛ avocado	1 Vegetable 2 Fat	1 cup salad with 1 Tbsp low-fat dressing and ⅛ avocado	1 Vegetable 2 Fat
	12 grapes	1 Fruit	12 grapes	1 Fruit	12 grapes	1 Fruit	12 grapes	1 Fruit
Snack	½ serving Baked Tortilla Chips (page 62)	0.65 Grain 0.4 Fat	Baked Tortilla Chips (page 62)	1.3 Grain 0.8 Fat	Baked Tortilla Chips (page 62)	1.3 Grain 0.8 Fat	Baked Tortilla Chips (page 62)	1.3 Grain 0.8 Fat

	Plan 1		Plan 2		Plan 3		Plan 4	
Dinner	Mango Black Bean Salsa (page 169)	1 Fruit	Mango Black Bean Salsa (page 169)	1 Fruit	Mango Black Bean Salsa (page 169)	1 Fruit	Mango Black Bean Salsa (page 169)	1 Fruit
	Pasta Salad with Shrimp (page 120)	1 Grain 0.25 Vegetable 1.7 Protein 0.4 Fat	Pasta Salad with Shrimp (page 120)	1 Grain 0.25 Vegetable 1.7 Protein 0.4 Fat	2 servings Pasta Salad with Shrimp (page 120)	2 Grain 0.5 Vegetable 3.4 Protein 0.8 Fat	2 servings Pasta Salad with Shrimp (page 120)	2 Grain 0.5 Vegetable 3.4 Protein 0.8 Fat
	Gingery Sugar Snap Peas (page 153)	1 Vegetable	1½ servings Gingery Sugar Sugar Snap Peas (page 153)	1.5 Vegetable	2 servings Gingery Sugar Snap Peas (page 153)	2 Vegetable	2 servings Gingery Sugar Snap Peas (page 153)	2 Vegetable
	Individual Apple Crumble (page 185)	0.5 Grain 1.6 Fruit 0.2 Fat	Individual Apple Crumble (page 185)	0.5 Grain 1.6 Fruit 0.2 Fat	Individual Apple Crumble (page 185)	0.5 Grain 1.6 Fruit 0.2 Fat	Individual Apple Crumble (page 185)	0.5 Grain 1.6 Fruit 0.2 Fat
	8 ounces nonfat milk	1 Milk	8 ounces nonfat milk	1 Milk	8 ounces nonfat milk	1 Milk	8 ounces nonfat milk	1 Milk
Food group totals		5.65 Grain 4.8 Protein 2.2 Milk 4.1 Fruit 2.75 Vegetable 3.8 Fat		6.3 Grain 4.8 Protein 2.2 Milk 4.6 Fruit 3.25 Vegetable 5.2 Fat		7.3 Grain 6.5 Protein 3.2 Milk 4.6 Fruit 4 Vegetable 5.6 Fat		8.8 Grain 6.6 Protein 3.4 Milk 4.6 Fruit 4 Vegetable 6 Fat

INDEX

About the Authors

NAOMI NEUFELD, MD, FACE, has been working with overweight children and their families for more than 25 years. She is the founder and director of KidShape and an attending physician and former director of pediatric endocrinology at Cedars-Sinai Medical Center and Clinical Professor of Pediatrics at the UCLA School of Medicine. She is deeply involved in research into the causes of and cures for childhood and adolescent obesity. For more information on Naomi Neufeld and KidShape, visit www.kidshape.com.

DAVID LAWRENCE is a private family chef and caterer in Los Angeles specializing in innovative, healthy, palate-pleasing meals. Some of his fondest memories are of his mother cooking for friends and family, and he learned early the simple pleasure of setting out platters of food. Many chefs make cooking look like fun, but David makes it look like play. He says, "My goal is to make really great food that people can enjoy and to take the fear or mystique out of getting in the kitchen to make yourself something to eat." You'll find his Web site at www.chefdavidlawrence.com.

SARA J. HENRY is the author of *Arthritis: What You Need to Know* (Johns Hopkins Health) and coauthor of *The Little Blue Book of Fitness and Health* (Rutledge Hill Press) and *New Hope for People with Lupus* (Prima Publishing). She is a former writer and editor at Rodale Books, and has a passion for cycling, hiking, running, kayaking, and skiing.